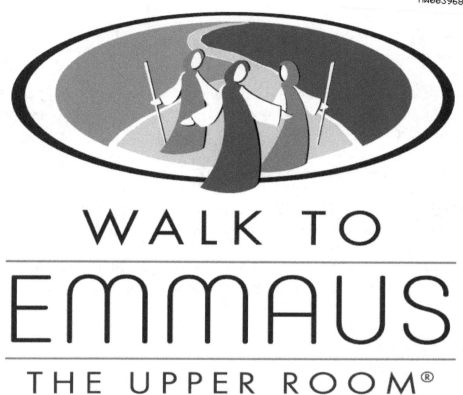

WALK TO
EMMAUS
THE UPPER ROOM®

DIRECTORS' MANUAL

UPPER
ROOM BOOKS®
NASHVILLE

**For more information about The Walk to Emmaus
or to learn about other Emmaus Ministries resources**
see emmaus.upperroom.org/
or call the International Emmaus Ministries Office
at (877) 899-2780 ext.7113 or (615) 340-7113.

CONTENTS

SECTION 1— THE EMMAUS MINISTRIES FAMILY

PURPOSE

Emmaus Ministries exists to inspire, challenge, and equip local faith communities for Christian action in their homes, churches, communities, and places of work. This purpose does not come to full realization for its participants during the Emmaus Ministries event itself but in the many days that follow.

Emmaus Ministries expands participants' spiritual lives, deepens their faith and discipleship, and rekindles—or perhaps ignites for the first time—their gifts as Christian leaders for their churches and communities. These aims are accomplished not only during the Emmaus Ministries event itself but also through participation in follow-up spiritual support groups and Community fellowship opportunities, sponsorship, prayer, support of other Emmaus Ministries events, and service on support committees and on teams.

Persons whose spiritual lives are renewed and strengthened through Emmaus Ministries are called and empowered to be the hands and feet of Christ: to share within their communities the grace they received. They become energetic and renewing catalysts in their homes, places of work or education, and local communities of faith. While walking together with other Christians, they actively participate in God's mission to the world.

HISTORY AND SCOPE

Emmaus Ministries includes programs for those seeking spiritual formation in several different life-stages:

- **Chrysalis** serves secondary (high school) young persons fifteen to eighteen years old;
- **Journey to the Table** serves young adults eighteen to thirty-five years old;
- **Walk to Emmaus** serves adults eighteen years and older;
- **Face to Face** serves adults sixty years and older.

Origins of the Ministries

Traditionally, in Christianity, a "three-day movement" was a movement that conducted spiritual renewal events and led by persons who had attended such an event. All such organizations were often collectively referred to as "three-day movements."

Most, but not all, of the events held by these organizations covered three days, and so the *Fourth Day* has become a term used by three-day movements to describe the life of the participant after the event.

The original three-day movement, Cursillo (cur-SEE-yoh), began in the Roman Catholic Church in Majorca, Spain, in 1944. Over time, Cursillo inspired the development of the Emmaus Ministries family of "three-day movement" programs.

Several resources provide information about the history of the Emmaus three-day movement and its relationship to Cursillo: *Day Four: The Pilgrim's Continued Journey, What Is Emmaus?*, and *The Early History of the Walk to Emmaus*.

In 1976, Danny Morris, Director of Developing Ministries for The Upper Room, participated in a Lutheran Cursillo in Florida and recognized the need for an ecumenical offering of Cursillo. On the same weekend, Maxie Dunnam, then World Editor of The Upper Room, participated in a prayer retreat at First United Methodist Church in Peoria, Illinois, where Cursillo participants served as table servants at the retreat. Their spiritual presence about the tables profoundly affected him.

Together, Danny and Maxie began to take steps toward including Cursillo as an Upper Room program. Under the leadership of Reverend Robert Wood, The Upper Room's first two model Cursillo weekends were held in Peoria, Illinois, in 1977. In 1978, Rev. Wood joined the staff of The Upper Room to launch the new Upper Room Cursillo movement.

In 1981, by mutual agreement with the National Secretariat of the Roman Catholic Cursillo, holder of the copyright to the Cursillo program, The Upper Room Cursillo became The Upper Room Walk to Emmaus. This change came about due to The Upper Room's call to be an ecumenical movement. The Upper Room reached an agreement with the National Cursillo Secretariat to develop a new program based on Cursillo but with distinctive leadership resources. Further, The Upper Room agreed not to use the traditional Cursillo language derived from its Spanish origin. The Upper Room developed The Walk to Emmaus design, talk outlines, and leadership manuals for use by an ecumenical audience.

Chrysalis began in 1984 in response to numerous requests from Emmaus Ministries Communities for a version of the Walk to Emmaus specifically for high school students. The Walk to Emmaus and TEC (Teens Encounter Christ—the youth expression of the Roman Catholic Cursillo) influenced the early development of Chrysalis. A group of Nashville high school youth attended TEC and acted as advisers to The Upper Room staff in creating a unique model and name for the program. And then, in 1989, The Upper Room and the Alabama/West Florida Emmaus Community sponsored the first Chrysalis event for college-age young people.

Face to Face, an adaptation of The Walk to Emmaus, was developed to meet the needs and life stages of older adults and those for whom an overnight experience presented a challenge.

Development of the Face to Face program began in 2008, with the first Encounter being held in 2011 in a Nashville area church. In 2014, the first Encounter using the officially developed materials took place and in 2015 Emmaus Ministries Communities outside the Nashville area began to hold Encounters.

Journey to the Table had its beginning in March of 2014, when The Upper Room established a new staff position for "Young Adult Spiritual Development." In September of 2014, the first five steering team leaders came to Nashville for three days of prayerful discussion and planning. After that meeting, an additional fourteen people joined working groups to write the first draft of the program. This group included young adults, campus ministers, and Emmaus and Chrysalis leaders. That draft of the new Journey to the Table program was completed in March of 2015, and five locations held test events in 2015 and 2016. The official launch of the program was held at The Upper Room in Nashville, Tennessee, in July 2016.

Keeping Faith with the Emmaus Program Models

Shared Experience

By participating in any of these ministries, the Community shares in a common experience with participants and teams around the world. Communities that remain healthy and fruitful over time demonstrate a commitment to this shared experience. This commitment helps leaders focus on the basics of providing a spiritual formation experience and connect all people involved through their shared experience. Persons can sponsor family and friends in other states, even in other countries, with confidence that the quality of the event will be the same in each location. Church leaders in one part of a country can recommend Emmaus Ministries events to church leaders in another part of the country, knowing that the design and standards remain uniform everywhere.

The Upper Room Emmaus Ministries office works with a Vision Team of experienced leaders in these ministries to review and revise the manuals. When Communities envision a new or revised element of one of these ministries, please consult with The Upper Room Emmaus Ministries office.

Faithfulness to The Upper Room Emmaus Ministries' program manuals affects the ongoing quality and effectiveness of Emmaus programs for the following reasons:

- **It prevents redesign by each leader.** Adherence to the manuals prevents individual leaders from redesigning Emmaus events according to their whims. Unlike many religious events, Emmaus is not leader-centered: Its effectiveness does not depend on particular charismatic personalities, gifted presenters, or experienced retreat masters. No one asks, when invited to attend an Emmaus event, who the leader and speakers will be. Rather, Emmaus depends on a team of committed Christians working together in the spirit of Christ according to directions in objective manuals based on a proven model. The event team leaders for each Emmaus event are accountable to the local Emmaus Board, and the local Board covenants with Upper Room Emmaus Ministries to lead the events according to the manuals.

- **It assures consistent quality and common experience.** The manuals ensure that Emmaus, no matter where it is conducted, will be a common and trustworthy experience. Persons can sponsor family and friends in other states, even in other countries, with confidence that the quality of the event will be the same in each location. Church leaders in one part of a country can recommend Emmaus events to church leaders in another part of the country, knowing that the design and standards are uniform everywhere. This uniformity strengthens the Emmaus movement and its value to the church.

- **It honors the integrity of the sponsors.** Persons come to an Emmaus event trusting others' recommendation that Emmaus will be worth their time and will be conducted according to a certain design. Therefore, Emmaus leaders honor sponsors' faith that the event team will offer the program's model in its integrity.

- **It preserves an organic model.** The Emmaus manuals set forth program models in which all parts are theologically and dynamically congruent. All Emmaus events are tightly woven. The models have proven their value and effectiveness time and again as instruments of the Holy Spirit in the lives of the participants and the churches to which they belong. Every part of the models has its purpose in this regard. When leaders rearrange a program model, adding some parts and deleting others, they increasingly diminish the model's potential for working as a whole to communicate the Christian message on many levels.

- **It serves as a shared and stabilizing discipline.** Commitment to the manuals is a shared discipline that serves as a check on the inclination of team members to innovate and tinker with the design. In truth, most additions and changes are made for the team, not the participants. Team leaders may be motivated by a desire to replicate a spontaneous happening from a previous event or to add an experience from a retreat they once attended. Or they may get bored with the same routine and desire to try out a few ideas of their own. Some leaders have a gift for designing learning experiences and retreats; they may feel confident that they can improve Emmaus Ministries program, given an opportunity. Emmaus Ministries programs, however, already includes more content than any participant can absorb over the course of the event; it offers enough material to meditate on for several years. Emmaus Ministries program do not need to include every meaningful experience, interesting retreat idea, or variation from other spiritual events. Nor can Emmaus Ministries expand to meet every need in a participant's life. The church and the Emmaus Fourth Day follow-up activities provide other opportunities for spiritual renewal that can creatively support and challenge a participant's faith. Not everything that is meaningful has to happen during the Emmaus Ministries event itself.

- **It channels creativity appropriately.** The manuals encourage leaders to focus their creativity on the given tasks within the Emmaus Ministries models. The place for creativity is not in redesigning the models but in making the most of the given designs to prepare the way of the Lord for the participants. The structure of Emmaus Ministries does not crowd out the Holy Spirit. Rather, it creates trustworthy space for the Holy Spirit to work in the midst of participants by eliminating anxiety about the weekend design and relaxing the focus on leaders. Acceptance of the models and manuals frees the event teams to focus on the participants and to trust the Holy Spirit. In addition, changes by independent-minded team members set a dangerous precedent. While their innovations may work, future teams will want to claim their right to be creative as well and to try out their own ideas. Even more serious, changes become traditions overnight because new Emmaus Community members believe their experience represents the true Emmaus model. The manuals are the plumb line that keeps each event centered on the prescribed program.

- **It prevents conflict over the event design.** The discipline of adhering to the manuals frees the Emmaus Board and teams to focus their energies in the proper direction—on preparing for Emmaus events and Fourth Day challenges. Well-designed and carefully tested programs with complete materials for leading them is a gift that frees Emmaus Communities to get on with the business at hand.

- **It enables Emmaus Communities to participate more fully in the larger Emmaus movement.** Emmaus Communities that are grounded in The Upper Room Emmaus Ministries models have the privilege and ability to be asked to work with The Upper Room Emmaus Ministries to help start new Emmaus groups and ministries. The Upper Room Emmaus Ministries Office seeks Emmaus leaders and Communities that know and practice the Emmaus Ministries models and want to help spread Emmaus in a trustworthy and dependable manner.

- **It honors the covenant with Upper Room Emmaus Ministries.** The manuals warrant adherence because an Emmaus Community exists through a covenant with The Upper Room Emmaus Ministries Office. As a condition of that covenant, each Emmaus Community agrees to follow the manuals. No doubt, other practices, including other three-day movement experiences, are rich and meaningful. Affirming the Emmaus models does not negate the validity of other promising experiences. However, if a group has decided to be an Emmaus Community, then that decision dictates that the Community be true to its identity and present the distinctive Emmaus Ministries models. Emmaus Communities function under the banner of The Upper Room Emmaus Ministries and are responsible for doing so in a manner faithful to the conditions of that relationship.

- **Change should be in the direction of moving closer to The Upper Room model.** Each Emmaus Community has its own personality and style. The Upper Room Emmaus Ministries Office will work with international Communities based on their cultures to ensure that they adhere to the basic Emmaus model. Minor differences will exist among some Communities because of their regions and background in starting. This will always be the case and is more noticeable in some areas than in others. But the direction of change for an Emmaus Community's models should always be in the direction of the standard Upper Room Emmaus Ministries models, not away from them.

The appropriate way to channel concerns and suggestions for improving the basic Emmaus programs' models and manuals is through The Upper Room Emmaus Ministries Office and the Emmaus Ministries Vision Team. The Vision Team consists of experienced, grassroots Emmaus Ministries leaders from Communities across the Emmaus movement. Emmaus Communities work with The Upper Room Emmaus Ministries Office to make improvements based on adequate understanding of and experience with the basic Emmaus Ministries models. Each Emmaus Community functions beyond its local group; each Community is part of a larger Emmaus Ministries movement.

SECTION 2—LAY DIRECTOR

The Lay Director is the principal layperson responsible to the Board for

- assembling the Walk team,
- guiding the team's weeks of preparation for the Walk,
- and directing the activities during the Walk.

The Emmaus Board prayerfully selects the Lay Director for this significant position of servant leadership.

The Lay Director and the Spiritual Director are partners in ministry. The Assistant Lay Directors support and aid the Lay Director's leadership and learn from the Lay Director how to lead future Walks. The Lay Director relies on God, the prayers of the Emmaus community members, the support of the board, and guidance and encouragement of past Lay Directors as he or she fulfills the responsibilities of the role.

QUALIFICATIONS

The Board of Directors selects the Lay Director based on his or her spiritual and technical readiness for the role of forming a team and acting as the public leader of the Walk. The Lay Director's experience will include having served Emmaus in background roles and on Conference Room Teams in a variety of positions. He or she will have served as an Assistant Lay Director more than once. This role requires spiritual maturity and active participation in a local church and an accountability group. Obviously, the Lay Director is willing and available to commit the time to plan and lead team meetings, the Walk, and to attend the Fourth Day Follow-up Meeting along with the Assistant Lay Directors.

RESPONSIBILITIES

The Lay Director leads team members through team formation; oversees the conducting of the Walk; and, with the team, attends the Fourth-Day Follow-up Meeting as a witness and as affirmation to the Walk participants. The Lay Director holds a final team meeting (in conjunction with the Fourth Day Follow-Up Meeting or at a later time) to facilitate an evaluation of the Walk.

During Team Formation

The Lay Director's most important job, in concert with the Spiritual Director, is to build and prepare the team so its members model and display Christian community. In other words, the Lay Director orchestrates the development of all parts of the team and the Walk into an integrated whole. If prepared properly, the Lay Director does not need to check on every detail during the Walk itself. He or she can trust and support other team members as they do their jobs.

During the Walk

The Lay Director has weighty responsibility during the Walk. The Lay Director (with the Spiritual Director's support) directs the activities, following the 3-Day Schedule. If timing gets off schedule, the Lay Director decides how to make up the time. During the Walk, the Lay Director leads team meetings for the Conference Room Team. When problems arise with participants, the Lay Director, along with the Spiritual Director, attends to those needs. By sharing responsibilities effectively with the Assistant Lay Directors, the Lay Director can concentrate on the dynamics of the conference room and participant responses. Finally, the Lay Director gives the PERSEVERANCE talk; the rationale behind the Lay Director's giving this talk is explained in the "Team Selection and Talk Assignments" section of this manual.

The Walk is harvest time after weeks of preparation. The success of the Walk largely depends on the groundwork of the preceding weeks of team meetings.

Servant Leader

The Lay Director's leadership of the team exudes confidence and firmness without being authoritarian. He or she leads by serving. The role of the Lay Director is that of a shepherd— guiding and directing with care, confidence, and creativity.

The Lay Director acts under the authority of the Emmaus Board. The Walk does not belong to the Lay Director! The Lay Director leads the Walk on behalf of the Board and under the agreement with The Upper Room so that the Walk can serve God's intention for the pilgrims.

Following the guidance of the *Emmaus Ministries Community Manual* and this *Walk to Emmaus Directors' Manual* provides a valuable key to success for the Walk itself and for the Community. The common goal of the Board of Directors and the Lay Director is to build continuity from one Emmaus event to another. Faithful adherence to the manuals from one event to the next builds confidence and trust in the Emmaus program. The Holy Spirit works through the team and the framework of Emmaus to enliven the experience and open the hearts of the participants to God.

The Upper Room expects that Communities will conduct Emmaus events in accordance with its published guidelines, thus maintaining the singular theme of Emmaus: The story found in Luke 24:13-35. Such compliance also eliminates potential complications. When Lay Directors establish an overlay of additional themes, these additions can obscure the primary image that guides the Emmaus event. Efforts by speakers to incorporate secondary themes into their talks can further complicate the message and hinder speaker preparation.

Competition among Lay Directors for the most creative themes distracts the community and does not serve the pilgrims.

Laity and Clergy in Partnership

Emmaus depends on the partnership of laity and clergy in ministry. In Emmaus, laypersons carry primary responsibility for the structure, functional aspects, and flow of an event. They work with clergy to ensure the spiritual integrity of the experience. Emmaus revitalizes and empowers the laity as the people of God by taking their commitment, maturity, and gifts for Christian service seriously.

Emmaus intends balance rather than dominance by either laity or clergy. The Emmaus design fosters and models a partnership between laity and clergy in the work of the church, and both groups benefit from participating in this experience. Leadership roles on Emmaus events and in the Emmaus Community require both laity and clergy, which characterize Emmaus as a spiritual renewal movement within the church.

To achieve a sense of shared leadership during team formation and the entire Emmaus event, the Lay Director builds a good working relationship with the Spiritual Director. Including the Spiritual Director and Assistant Spiritual Directors in creative planning lightens the load and enhances the spiritual quality of many aspects of Emmaus. Involved and informed Spiritual Directors can bring wisdom and experience to difficult situations that may arise during the Walk. The interaction and collaboration among the Lay Director, Spiritual Director, and Assistant Spiritual Directors greatly affect the meaningful involvement of clergy and their desire to participate in Emmaus leadership roles.

LAY DIRECTOR'S CHECKLIST

Before the Walk

1. Accept the Emmaus Board's invitation to serve as Lay Director for the Walk only after prayer and reflection on the required commitment.

2. Meet with the Team Selection Committee (and the Spiritual Director) to select potential team members. (See the "Team Selection" section in this manual.)

   a) Contact the chair of the Team Selection Committee and Spiritual Director to set a meeting date as soon as possible.

   b) Pray about recommendations for potential team members before presenting them to the Team Selection Committee.

3. Meet with the Spiritual Director to begin the team-building process: establish team meeting dates, clarify each other's roles for team meetings, and chart the prayer partners on the worksheet found in this manual (see the "Team Meeting Forms and Handouts" section in this manual).

   a) Call and invite laypeople whom the Team Selection Committee select to serve on the team; the Spiritual Director will call and invite the clergypersons selected.

b) Call the designated member of the Team Selection Committee to discuss other prospects if you have problems completing your team assignments.

c) Finalize the team roster and give copies to the Team Selection chair to share with the board and the communications team.

d) Mail a "welcome to the team" letter to each team member and enclose a team meeting schedule, team roster, talk and prayer schedule, and talk outline (as appropriate) or appropriate checklist.

e) Prepare a schedule of talk previews, prayer partner assignments, a plan for refreshments, the meeting format, other handouts, and specific instructions to Assistant Lay Directors about roles and duties at team meetings for the first team meeting. Keep in mind that the Lay Director takes responsibility to train leadership for future Walk events.

4. Build and prepare the team through a series of well-planned team meetings.

a) Lead the team meetings with the supportive involvement of the Spiritual Director and the help of the Assistant Lay Directors and Assistant Spiritual Directors.

b) Include in team meetings the elements in the section on team formation (in this manual): Begin meetings with worship and "floating" accountability groups; provide instruction on Walk dynamics; preview talks; train Table Leaders.

c) Meet separately with the Assistant Lay Directors to review and clarify their responsibilities on the Walk and to adjust the Walk schedule as needed to maintain the rhythm of the Walk.

5. Contact all support committee chairs to make sure their understanding of their responsibilities matches the team's expectations. Encourage these persons in their work without doing their jobs for them. That frees you from distraction, allows you rest before the Walk, or gives others opportunities to serve.

6. Prepare and preview Talk #14, PERSEVERANCE.

During the Walk

1. Conduct the Walk according to the *Emmaus Ministries Community Manual* and this *Walk to Emmaus Directors' Manual*.

a) Give Talk #14, PERSEVERANCE.

b) Make sure at least two leaders remain at the leaders' table when pilgrims are in the Conference Room.

c) Hold team meetings at least on Thursday and Friday nights of the Walk; invite team members to share celebrations from the day as well as general concerns. (Team members share specific concerns only with the Spiritual Director or with you.)

d) Rely upon the Assistant Lay Directors to carry the bulk of the responsibilities during the Walk, thereby training them in leadership for future Walks. Stay in close and cooperative communication with the Spiritual Director.

After the Walk

1. Participate in the Fourth Day Follow-up Meeting with the pilgrims and team.

2. Hold a final team meeting to evaluate the Walk to learn from mistakes, to celebrate victories, and to suggest improvement to the Board of Directors. Coordinate with the Board Representative in preparing an evaluation report to submit to the board.

SECTION 3—
ASSISTANT LAY
DIRECTORS

RESPONSIBILITIES

The Assistant Lay Directors carry a considerable load for the team. Their primary responsibility comes in helping the Lay Director prepare the team prior to the Walk and to keep the Walk running smoothly and on schedule. As much as possible, Assistant Lay Directors free the Lay Director from concern for details so that he/she can give attention to the team, pilgrims, and overall progress of the Walk. The Assistant Lay Directors serve as the timekeepers for the Walk, and they anticipate preparation for each aspect of the Walk.

ASSISTANT LAY DIRECTORS' CHECKLIST

Before the Walk

1. Assistant Lay Directors meet with the Lay Directors to

   a) Review responsibilities and discuss their helpfulness to the Lay Director.

   b) Begin to work out the duties for each Assistant Lay Director during team formation and the Walk.

   c) Develop the agenda for team meetings, being careful to include team and Table Leader training.

2. Prepare your talk for preview. If your talk is PRIORITY and is the first talk previewed, serve as a model for future previews. If your talk is FOURTH DAY, be certain your personal practices accurately and authentically represent the Fourth Day emphases of the Community.

3. Assist the Lay Director in leading team meetings.

   a) Arrive early to set up the meeting room; have routine supplies, such as name tags, available for each meeting.

   b) Keep the talk preview session on schedule as agreed upon with the Lay Director. This offers excellent practice for the actual Walk.

   c) Assist speakers with visual components in cooperation with the Media Servant, if there is one.

d) Escort speakers out of the room following a preview, and remain with them during discussion time.

4. Help build a sense of community.

   a) Get to know all team members.

   b) Make yourself available to team members, especially first timers, to help with talks, offer support, and share ideas.

   c) Encourage a spirit of agape and prayer by example.

   d) Serve other team members at all times.

5. Before the Walk, meet with the Lay Director and the Spiritual Director to review every aspect of the Walk schedule.

   a) Share suggestions for team table assignments with the Lay Director.

   b) Be sure responsibilities for the duration of the Walk are clear and concise.

   c) Ask questions and clarify any remaining logistics of the Walk.

During the Walk

1. Carry out assignments throughout the Walk according to the Lay Director's agreement with the Assistant Lay Directors. The responsibilities are generally grouped in this way:

   a) One Assistant Lay Director works in the Conference Room as timekeeper, shares the job of introducing talks with the Lay Director, and monitors the flow of the Walk according to the Walk Schedule.

   b) A second Assistant Lay Director notifies speakers to get dressed, accompanies them to the chapel, joins others to pray for the speakers, returns to the chapel with speakers after their talk for additional prayer, and helps present general agape letters and banners.

   c) A third Assistant Lay Director runs errands, finds stragglers, helps present general agape and banners, and escorts table groups to the chapel for prayer.

   The Lay Director may ask the Assistant Lay Directors to rotate area responsibilities daily to enhance their learning and experience.

2. Give the PRIORITY or FOURTH DAY talk and fulfill jobs as assigned.

3. Follow the Walk Schedule closely while being flexible for special needs and a sense of natural flow. (See "Keeping the Schedule" in the "General Reminders" section of the *Emmaus Ministries Community Manual*.)

4. Serve as the liaison with behind-the-scenes support persons. (Fill in names of these persons in the chart on the following page.)

After the Walk

Participate in the Fourth-Day Follow-Up Meeting and the final team meeting to evaluate the Walk.

Behind-the-Scenes Support Roles

Kitchen Coordinator _____

_____

Prayer Chapel Coordinator _____

_____

Agape Food Coordinator _____

_____

Table Agape Coordinator _____

_____

Prayer Vigil Coordinator _____

_____

Permission is granted to duplicate this page.

SECTION 4— SPIRITUAL DIRECTOR

The Spiritual Director serves as the primary clergy leader of the Walk. Along with the Lay Director, the Spiritual Director properly prepares the team and conducts the Walk according to The Upper Room model. While the Spiritual Director and Lay Director work as partners in leadership, the Spiritual Director plays a support role in relation to the Lay Director in team formation and during the Walk. This approach develops and emphasizes the importance of lay leadership in Emmaus.

QUALIFICATIONS

The Board of Directors selects the Spiritual Director with recommendations from the Community Spiritual Director. This role requires Emmaus experience and training. Find detailed information about Spiritual Director's qualifications and responsibilities in the *Emmaus Ministries Community Manual* and in the book *Spiritual Directors*.

Ideally, a Spiritual Director has given all the clergy talks on previous Walks except MEANS OF GRACE. At a minimum, however, the Spiritual Director will have served an entire Walk in residence on an Emmaus team as an Assistant Spiritual Director at least once under the leadership of an experienced Spiritual Director. Beyond this, Communities may set standards for the further preparation of their Spiritual Directors.

The Spiritual Director will give the MEANS OF GRACE talk; the "Team Selection and Talk Assignments" section of this manual explains the rationale behind this choice. A Spiritual Director will also have demonstrated a commitment to team formation, give evidence of spiritual maturity as one in active ministry, and understand the nature and purpose of Emmaus in relation to the church. This person actively supports the Emmaus community and practices the Fourth Day disciplines. The role of Spiritual Director requires authorization to administer the sacrament of Holy Communion in the Emmaus setting. Like the Lay Director, the Spiritual Director commits to participate in all team meetings, the entire duration of the Walk, and Fourth Day Follow-Up meeting afterward.

RESPONSIBILITIES

The Spiritual Director, along with the Community Spiritual Director, has the primary responsibility for recruiting and training other clergy for spiritual leadership within the Emmaus movement. This responsibility includes ensuring that all Assistant Spiritual Directors have the skills and training needed to provide pastoral, theological, and spiritual guidance to the pilgrims and team members in this ecumenical movement. The Spiritual Director gives attention to the crucial roles of each Assistant Spiritual Director. The Spiritual Director requests maximum participation from each Assistant Spiritual Director and confirms that two of the four are consciously preparing for future leadership as a Spiritual Director.

The Spiritual Director serves as a pastor-at-large for the team during team formation and for the pilgrims during the Walk, working with the Lay Director and Assistant Spiritual Directors to guarantee that the process of team formation and talk preparation equips and spiritually enriches team members. The Spiritual Director and Assistant Spiritual Directors also exercise special care for the theological integrity of the talks during team formation and for the Walk.

In the book *Spiritual Directors,* the author emphasizes two important points: "Spiritual directors are available [during] the Emmaus [Walk] for holy listening," and "The intention of spiritual direction is to engage an individual in conversation about God's presence and calling in his or her life" (pp. 8, 9).

The Spiritual Director has knowledge about the current legal and religious standards for handling cases of sexual abuse, harassment, suicide, and so forth. The Spiritual Director makes this information clear to each Assistant Spiritual Director and serves as a consultant for the entire team regarding any sensitive or confidential information that participants may share during the Walk.

SPIRITUAL DIRECTOR'S CHECKLIST

Before the Walk

1. Accept the board's invitation to be the Spiritual Director of the Walk after prayer and reflection on the commitment required.

2. Meet with the Lay Director and the Team Selection Committee to select potential team members.

    a) Come prepared to recommend four clergy for the team: at least one resident Assistant Spiritual Director and one clergy for each grace talk (other than MEANS OF GRACE). Keep in mind the need to develop new Spiritual Directors. Remember that the final decision belongs to the Team Selection Committee and the Emmaus Board of Directors.

3. Secure the acceptance of the Assistant Spiritual Directors for the team after approval of the proposed team member list. Communicate to the Lay Director the names of the clergy who have agreed to serve.

4. Assist the Lay Director in building and preparing the team.

a) Meet with the Lay Director to establish team meeting dates and formats and to decide mutually upon each other's roles in team meetings.

b) Discuss with the other clergy on the team their role as Assistant Spiritual Directors for the Walk: their talk assignments and the desire to have talks fully prepared and previewed at a team meeting; the significance of their participation in team meetings; times when each will help lead worship at team meetings; and the value of their presence on the Walk, especially on the day of their talk and after Candlelight.

c) Arrange ahead of time to have at least two Spiritual Directors present for the prayer time following Candlelight for prayer and spiritual counseling with the pilgrims.

d) Plan worship for the opening of each team meeting and involve the leadership of the Assistant Spiritual Directors and the Music Leader.

e) Provide an overview of the theological and spiritual dynamics of Emmaus and the role of the team for the first team-meeting orientation, or arrange for the Community Spiritual Director to do the overview, depending on the Community's practice.

f) Support actively the Lay Director's leadership of the team meetings and preparations for the Walk; help make the team-formation process spiritually enriching and a community-building experience.

g) Take special interest in the talk previews to ensure the theological integrity and clarity of the talks; when necessary, take time to meet with speakers who have trouble preparing their talks.

h) Be available throughout team formation as a Spiritual Director and pastor to the team members.

i) Prepare the MEANS OF GRACE talk and preview it at a team meeting, making sure that all Assistant Spiritual Directors are present at that meeting.

j) Review all the Spiritual Director assignments for the Walk and decide which of the Spiritual Director responsibilities to assign to Assistant Spiritual Directors. (See the "Spiritual Director's and Assistant Spiritual Directors' Assignment Worksheet" at the end of the "Assistant Spiritual Directors" section.)

During the Walk

Assist the Lay Director in conducting the Walk according to this *Emmaus Directors' Manual*.

1. Assume responsibility for presenting or preparing Assistant Spiritual Directors to present the Spiritual Director parts over the course of the Walk.

2. Present the MEANS OF GRACE talk during the Walk.

3. Make sure the Community Spiritual Director is prepared to present the Emmaus Cross to the Lay Director during the Closing and to lead the closing service of Holy Communion, or be prepared to do so yourself.

After the Walk

1. Attend the Fourth Day meeting with the pilgrims and team after the Walk, as well as the team evaluation meeting.

2. Communicate with pastors of the pilgrims, informing them of their members' participation in a Walk. A sample letter is provided (see the "Walk Spiritual Director's Letter to Participant's Pastor" on the following page).

   a) Normally, the Emmaus secretary or registrar will prepare these letters after the Thursday night Send-Off. The Spiritual Director signs the letters before Closing on Sunday. The signed letters are returned to the secretary or registrar, who will mail them on Monday.

   b) This procedure shifts the cost of producing and mailing the letters to the Emmaus Community rather than the Spiritual Director.

WALK SPIRITUAL DIRECTOR'S LETTER TO PARTICIPANT'S PASTOR

The Walk Spiritual Director sends this letter to a participant's pastor at the conclusion of the Walk. Revise to fit the circumstances of the Walk and your Community.

Dear Pastor,

I am pleased to inform you, as a colleague and as one who has had temporary pastoral care for a member of your congregation, that [Participant's Full Name] attended [Walk #] on [Walk Dates]. As you may know, [The Walk to Emmaus] is an Emmaus Ministry of The Upper Room and is held in our area at [Event Location].

Emmaus Ministry programs are designed to strengthen and renew the faith of its participants and, through them, to renew their families and congregations. An Emmaus event includes an experience of living in Christian community with daily prayer, Holy Communion, and discussion. The discussions take place around talks given by both laypersons and clergy on the theme of God's grace and how that grace comes alive in the Christian community and the world. Emmaus also includes an ongoing support program after the event.

As the [Walk]'s Spiritual Director, I encourage you to invite [Participant's First Name] to share what the [Event] meant to [him/her] and to discuss what [he/she] plans to do as a result. If a personal conversation is not possible, you can show your support and openness to [Participant's First Name]'s experience by sending [him/her] a card of congratulations for having attended. You could call or email to let [him/her] know you are aware of [his/her] participation. This will allow you to guide [him/her] into the most appropriate ways that this experience can translate into servant leadership within your congregation and the larger body of Christ. The purpose of Emmaus is to strengthen the church. [Participant's First Name] may need your help to bridge the gap between the event experience and the post-event challenge of living out the faith.

Some people come away from their [Walk] with great zeal and new priorities for their lives. Others come away feeling strengthened and confirmed in an already rich and lively faith. It seems that most everyone comes away having experienced God's love in Christ and desiring to pass it on in daily life. Many need their pastor to guide them in the best ways to grow this love.

If you have questions or concerns, please feel free to contact me or one of the other local clergy leaders in Emmaus: [Names & Phone Numbers of Emmaus Spiritual Directors].

Grace and peace,

[Walk Spiritual Director's Name]
[Walk] Spiritual Director, [Community Name] Emmaus Community
[Walk] Spiritual Director's Phone Number

Permission is granted to duplicate this letter.

SECTION 5— ASSISTANT SPIRITUAL DIRECTORS

The Assistant Spiritual Directors help the Spiritual Director carry out the clergy assignments and responsibilities, provide spiritual guidance, and offer a pastoral presence on the Walk. For this reason, Assistant Spiritual Directors review the role and responsibilities of the Spiritual Director as described in the previous section.

QUALIFICATIONS

An Assistant Spiritual Director shall be a clergyperson engaged in ministry and have the appropriate credentials within his or her respective tradition. He or she has attended an Emmaus or similar three-day movement event, supports the Emmaus community actively, and practices Fourth Day disciplines.

Detailed information about Assistant Spiritual Directors' qualifications and responsibilities can be found in the *Emmaus Ministries Community Manual* and in the book *Spiritual Directors*.

RESPONSIBILITIES

Before the Walk

Assistant Spiritual Directors commit to participate in as many team meetings and as much of the Walk as possible or to an extent negotiated with the Spiritual Director and Lay Director.

Assistant Spiritual Directors preview assigned talks during team meetings and improve their presentations based on feedback from the team members. They also actively participate in previewing the talks of other team members, especially the Spiritual Director and other Assistant Spiritual Directors.

Assistant Spiritual Directors share leadership for worship and Holy Communion at team meetings in cooperation with the Spiritual Director. Like the Spiritual Director, Assistant Spiritual Directors support team leaders in the team-building process by modeling a servant spirit and enhancing team formation as an opportunity for leadership development.

During the Walk

During the Walk, each Assistant Spiritual Director presents an assigned talk and assists the Spiritual Director with other assignments, such as morning and evening meditations and spiritual guidance after Candlelight. Assistant Spiritual Directors may make themselves available to pray with speakers before and after the speakers' talks.

Assistant Spiritual Directors commit to stay with the team during the duration of the Walk or for as much of the Walk as possible so that pilgrims have plenty of opportunities to receive spiritual guidance and support. Qualified Assistant Spiritual Directors receive training as potential Spiritual Directors for future Walks. The team expects Assistant Spiritual Directors to make every effort to be present for the full day on which they present their talks, for spiritual guidance after the Dying Moments Communion Service, for Candlelight, and for Closing.

SPIRITUAL DIRECTOR'S AND ASSISTANT SPIRITUAL DIRECTORS' ASSIGNMENT WORKSHEET

The Spiritual Director will encourage the four Assistant Spiritual Directors to participate in presenting the various meditations. For the pilgrims to know and trust the clergy leaders, it helps to have the Spiritual Director introduce the Saturday morning meditation and then allow each Assistant Spiritual Director to present one of the four responses to Christ. The team may use the same format for the Sunday morning meditation.

In the schedule that follows, the Spiritual Director makes the actual assignments for the weekend.

Thursday

__SD and ASD 1__	6:00 p.m.	Team Commissioning Service
__SD__		Comments before the Thursday night movie
__SD__		Summary after the movie

Friday

_____	7:00 a.m.	Communion liturgy
__ASD 1__		Meditation #1: THE LOVING FATHER (Prodigal Son)
__ASD 1__	1:45 p.m.	PREVENIENT GRACE talk
__ASD 2__	3:00 p.m.	JUSTIFYING GRACE talk
__ASD 2__	7:10 p.m.	Emmaus Road Prayer Experience
__SD__	10:00 p.m.	Examination of Conscience

Permission is granted to duplicate this page.

Saturday

1. _____

2. _____

    7:30 a.m.   Meditation #2: FOUR RESPONSES TO CHRIST

(SD introduces four responses; each ASD presents one response.) At a minimum, share the responsibility with other clergy who are training to be future Spiritual Directors.

3. _____

4. _____

_____SD_____   10:15 a.m.   MEANS OF GRACE talk

_____SD_____   11:45 a.m.   Dying Moments Communion Service

__SD and ASDs__   2:00 p.m.   Questions on MEANS OF GRACE talk

_____SD_____   2:25 p.m.   Introduce chapel visits by tables

_____ASD 3_____   4:30 p.m.   OBSTACLES TO GRACE talk

_____SD_____   10:00 p.m.   Explanation of Candlelight

_____SD_____   10:10 p.m.   Examination of Conscience

Sunday

__SD introduces__   7:30 a.m.   Meditation #3: THE HUMANNESS OF JESUS

(Address some of the following topics; include at least four.) At a minimum, share the responsibility with other clergy who are training to be future Spiritual Directors.

_____

_____

_____

_____

_____

_____

_____

_____

_____

- Jesus experienced disappointment
- Jesus experienced fatigue.
- Jesus experienced anger.
- Jesus experienced suffering.
- Jesus experienced love.
- Jesus experienced empathy.
- Jesus experienced and initiated human understanding.
- Jesus was firm.
- Jesus knew when to ask for support

Permission is granted to duplicate this page.

__ASD 4__	10:00 a.m.	SANCTIFYING GRACE talk
__SD__	3:00 p.m.	Reminders/check addresses of pilgrims
__SD__	3:30 p.m.	Introduction of agape letters
__SD and ASD 4__	4:15 p.m.	Cross commissioning service
__CSD*__	Introduce Lay Director at Closing and present cross.	
__CSD*__	Communion at Closing *(Note: Pilgrims' sharing serves as the meditation.)*	

Permission is granted to duplicate this page.

*Normally the Community Spiritual Director introduces the Lay Director and leads Communion during Closing. If the Community Spiritual Director is not available, the Walk Spiritual Director may lead Communion.

Key to Abbreviations

SD = Walk Spiritual Director

ASD = Assistant Spiritual Director

CSD = Community Spiritual Director

SECTION 6—
TABLE LEADERS AND ASSISTANT TABLE LEADERS

Table Leaders and Assistant Table Leaders are at the Walk to lead the pilgrims. They facilitate table interaction in response to each talk and support the building of *koinonia*—Christian community—among those at the table. In many respects, Table Leaders and Assistant Table Leaders have the most important responsibility in the conference room. The pilgrims experience most of the Walk and develop lasting relationships at the table.

The Lay Director recognizes the Table Leaders and Assistant Table Leaders as team members on Thursday evening. They are identified publicly on Friday morning as the table process is explained, the table assignments are made, and the pilgrims take a seat. The Table Leaders and Assistant Table Leaders also sit. They serve without distinction alongside the pilgrims and participate fully as table members.

Both the Table Leader and the Assistant Table Leader serve in their roles as friends among friends. Their leadership style is low-key but not invisible.

- A Table Leader who tries to remain invisible practices deception and may frustrate the table members and the process, especially when the table needs leadership or when pilgrims need to speak to a team member.

- The Assistant Table Leader supports the Table Leader by exemplifying full and cooperative participation with the other table members. The Assistant Table Leader may befriend withdrawn pilgrims and help create an accepting table family by being a caring presence as a table member rather than as a recognized leader.

Table Leaders and Assistant Table Leaders, like all team members, assume no special privileges over the pilgrims and always remember they are also pilgrims in need of God's grace and guidance. They take no false pride in the fact that they have been on a Walk (or served on teams) before; therefore, they do not talk about it unless asked.

Assistant Table Leaders need not be secretive or deceptive with the pilgrims about their team role. The challenge for Assistant Table Leaders is to be at one with them as pilgrims, humbly serving without calling attention to self.

The Assistant Table Leader's role is often a person's first Conference Room Team experience as he or she prepares to be a Table Leader on a subsequent Walk, but it is not limited to first-time team members. Sometimes it may be advantageous or necessary for the Assistant Table Leader to give a talk.

RESPONSIBILITIES

Set an Example

Table Leaders and Assistant Table Leaders guide by example; they set an example with their positive attitude. An attitude of confidence, interest, personal openness, and eager participation in every part of the Walk will encourage the openness and participation of the pilgrims as well. On the other hand, an attitude of boredom or constant fatigue will foster the same among the table members and reinforce the voices of apathy, lethargy, or cynicism among them.

Table Leaders and Assistant Table Leaders also set an example by being authentic. Their willingness to share life struggles and experiences gives others the freedom to be open and vulnerable as well. By being their honest selves about faith and experience with God, Table Leaders and Assistant Table Leaders give others the space to do likewise and to rediscover their own unique relationship with God. They are not teachers, group therapists, spiritual gurus, or table evangelists; they simply share themselves as persons living in God's accepting grace.

The Assistant Table Leaders guide by example not position. They serve as agents of God's love and support the Table Leader's initiatives. Their role provides an opportunity to serve and to grow in humility in the process.

Create a Caring, Affirming Atmosphere

Table Leaders' and Assistant Table Leaders' accepting attitude will foster acceptance among the table members as well. They want the table group to become the pilgrims' family for the weekend, a place where the pilgrims can be honest about feelings and can explore life experiences in relation to the talks and the Walk.

By giving personal attention to each member of the table community at different times throughout the three days, the Table Leader and Assistant Table Leader can foster an atmosphere of sensitivity and caring for one another. By involving withdrawn table members and by curbing those who tend to dominate, the Table Leader can make the table a place where all receive affirmation for who they are and for the gifts they bring to the table community.

Many times, Table Leaders can soften the domineering style of some table members by calling for and affirming responses from others deliberately, guarding each person's opportunity to speak or reminding table members to listen to one another's responses. Sometimes domineering pilgrims can become a positive presence through encouragement of their leadership potential or private requests to cooperate in drawing out another table member. Sometimes Table Leaders speak frankly though privately to domineering table members about the effect of their manner on table dynamics.

In some cases, a clergy person may become too involved in the dialogue at a particular table. This can be a teaching moment between the Weekend Spiritual Director and the clergy person. What is most important is the building of trust within that table community. Having someone who is an outsider, even if they have been called in for a specific point or question, interrupts that building process and should be avoided at all cost.

Guide Discussion Skillfully

Table Leaders offer discussion starters and the necessary direction to enable dialogue and table work. Some tables need little help discussing or working together; guidance may simply involve reminding the group to move on to summaries and representations of the summaries. Other tables require prompts with discussion questions that elicit responses from each person around the table: "What part of the talk got your attention the most and why?" Sometimes it helps to introduce a question by offering a personal response: "Out of all she said in her talk, the one thing I found most significant was . . . because. . . . What about each of you? What spoke to you?" "What do you think she was trying to say? How have you experienced that?" What about that is important to you? Why?"

Intentionality with questions is key. One experienced Table Leader said, "It never fails. I think up a couple of good, open questions while we listen to a talk and write them in my notes in preparation for the discussion. Then I use the questions to begin the discussion, and the discussion goes well. When I wing it and begin with a less focused question like, 'Well, what do you think?' the discussion is less likely to go anywhere." Table Leaders prime the pump with their own thoughtful questions.

Intentionality about listening to people's responses also creates a climate for good dialogue. Some people do not speak because they believe no one listens. Good questions may generate talk, but they cannot bring about dialogue unless persons actively listen to one another.

Encourage Self-Direction of the Table

Table Leaders lead by encouraging the healthy leadership and initiatives shown by the table members. The Table Leader guides discussion and table work until the group assumes ownership of the table community's life. The Table Leader works toward that end with an unassuming posture that evidences no need to be in charge. Table Leaders learn to guide without dominating or making themselves the center of the table's experience.

Prepare for Their Roles

Two resources will help teams understand the role and responsibilities of the Table Leader and Assistant Table Leader. The *Walk to Emmaus Team Manual* chapter on "Table Dynamics" provides a thorough discussion of the responsibilities of Table Leaders and Assistant Table Leaders and the attitudes and skills that help them do their jobs well. An appendix in the *Walk to Emmaus Team Manual* offers a Table Training, which includes presentation, discussion, and role play.

TABLE LEADERS' AND ASSISTANT TABLE LEADERS' CHECKLIST

Before the Walk

1. Participate fully in all team meetings in preparation for the Walk.
2. Prepare the talk for preview by the team if assigned a talk.

During the Walk

1. Lead the pilgrims throughout the Walk. Remain at the table during talk discussions, summaries, and summary representation times.

2. Notify an Assistant Lay Director for needed supplies or if a pilgrim leaves the table unexpectedly.

3. Present the talk as approved by the team if giving a talk during the Walk.

4. Prepare to guide the table discussion, summary, and summary response following the Table Leader's talk.

5. Remain seated in the same place while pilgrims rotate seats for each talk throughout the Walk. The Table Leader sits in the chair that puts his or her back to the speaker and faces toward the others at the table; the Assistant Table Leader sits on the opposite side. The two sit this way for the following reasons:

    *   It prevents the pilgrims from having to sit with their backs to the speaker.

    *   It allows the Table Leader to see the pilgrims and monitor their responses toward the talks and the Walk.

    *   It helps the others notice the Table Leader's example of paying attention and taking copious notes.

    *   It means that the Table Leader and Assistant Table Leader will have a chance to sit next to each pilgrim at the table.

    *   It allows each person at the table to participate from several different positions.

After the Walk

1. Participate in the Fourth Day Follow-Up Meeting and the final team meeting to evaluate the Walk.

2. A week or so after the Walk, reach out to the table group pilgrims with a card, a note, or a letter.

SECTION 7—MUSIC DIRECTORS

The Music Director and the Assistant Music Director are a vital part of the team and of the Emmaus experience. They provide the music during team meetings and for the entire Walk according to the Music Director's Checklist (at the end of this section). The ministry of music leadership for an Emmaus event calls for prayer, intentionality, and preparedness—it is not performance but humble servanthood as part of a team effort in God's service. For further insight about music on an Emmaus event, read the book *Music Directors and Song Leaders* before team meetings begin.

GENERAL REMINDERS

- Plan to attend every team meeting to help build the sense of community, provide music for team worship times, and practice music with the team.

- Familiarize yourself with the Walk site to obtain firsthand knowledge of the building, equipment (piano, organ, etc.), and locations for worship services.

- Study the Music Director's Checklist (found at the end of this section) and the Walk Schedule and take the initiative to plan music for the Walk.

- Meet with the Lay Director and Spiritual Director about the music plans. Consider their expectations and desires for music in team meetings and for the Walk.

- Use a variety of instruments for accompaniment (guitar, piano, rhythm instruments, and recorded accompaniment tracks).

- Balance familiar songs with new ones.

- Choose a balance of types of songs—lively songs, quiet songs, songs with or without hand motions, familiar hymns, camp songs, songs of praise, and songs of contrition. Diversity in music selections will better meet the needs and backgrounds of a variety of pilgrims and express more accurately the different moods of the Christian life. For example, praise songs alone do not help the pilgrims express their feelings of repentance or longing.

- Choose songs in advance and be ready to start before your scheduled time. If using instruments, tune them when the conference room is not in session. As soon as the Lay Director or Assistant Lay Director says to start, begin!

- Keep the pace moving. If leading the group in singing several songs, list titles (and page numbers if using songbooks) on the board or a large chart.

- Teach new songs after opening with a familiar song. Be sure you have practiced a new song so you can lead it. Do not teach new songs during worship; introduce the new songs earlier in preparation for worship times.

- Be ready for Communion services. Consult with the Spiritual Director about music plans and ask the following questions:

  - Where do you want music in the service?

  - Do you prefer certain songs, or shall I choose them?

  - Will we sing the Communion responses?

  - Do you want singing during the sharing of the bread and cup?

  - When will musicians take Communion?

- Be ready during worship times. Pauses break the flow and momentum unless intended for silence and reflection. When the liturgy includes a sung response, begin it without pause or comment. Lead from total preparation of body, mind, and spirit.

- Enjoy leading the music, and others will enjoy singing with you. Remember this: Your job is not to perform but to lead group singing.

- Meet with the Assistant Music Director to evaluate and plan together. You are the leader, but the Assistant Music Director can share in planning with you. Also consider where the Assistant Music Director or a third member of the music team can lead the group in singing or sing a solo. By doing this you prepare others for future leadership. Hold these meetings outside of team meeting time. During the Walk, meet when the conference room is not in session.

MUSIC ON A WALK

- Study and follow the Music Director's Checklist and the Walk Schedule.

- Remember that no group singing occurs on Thursday evening or early Friday morning.

- Prepare and practice for the meditative solos or duets used at the close of Thursday and Friday night prayer services and at the close of the prayer time following Candlelight if called for. The intent of the music is to enhance the meditations. Make solos quiet, reflective, and in no way a performance. The soloists sing from the back of the chapel, out of participants' sight.

- Teach the pilgrims "De Colores" and the table graces before the PREVENIENT GRACE talk on Friday morning. Share the traditions behind both practices as explained in the Music Director's Checklist.

- Teach the pilgrims "Jesus, Jesus" (only one stanza) on or before Saturday afternoon to prepare for Candlelight that night. "Jesus, Jesus" is a prayer song, not a song of encouragement or challenge. Educate the pilgrims and the team about the prayer song concept: a prayer song is more subdued and quiet and leads to an attitude or atmosphere of prayer.

- Teach other songs as needed.
- Lead singing whenever the Lay Director asks. Be ready with songs that are fun, lively, and involve movement. These songs help keep pilgrims alert.
- Be alert to the mood of the pilgrims. Be sensitive to when a prayer song, a fun song, or a praise song would be most appropriate.
- Be available to the table groups to assist with talk representations.
- Plan and lead music for Communion at the Closing if necessary.
- Maintain consistency between the gender of the music team and the gender of the pilgrims on the Walk.

MUSIC DIRECTOR'S SCHEDULE/CHECKLIST

Thursday

10:00 p.m.   Chapel—After the film, Spiritual Director's meditation, and Lay Director's comments, sing or play a meditative solo. The solo serves to enhance the meditation, which focuses on knowing self and where one is on the journey of faith.

Friday

11:00 A.M.   Teach the group a song (a possible selection is "Sing Alleluia to the Lord" from the pilgrims' worship booklet) to introduce talks, "De Colores" (worship booklet), and "Wesley's Grace" (worship booklet). The Music Director or Assistant Music Director explains the history of "De Colores" and the tradition of singing the blessing so pilgrims move beyond simply learning a song to participating in the history of the three-day movement.

- The song "De Colores" has a long-standing tradition in Emmaus and similar three-day programs. This song speaks of God's beauty in the world. According to tradition, people who had experienced the three-day short course in Christianity gave musical expression to their joy of God's love through the words of "De Colores." The words are sung to an old folk tune from Majorca, Spain.

- The tradition of singing grace before and after meals comes from the Benedictines who prayed God's blessing before the meal and thanked God for the blessing of the food and fellowship after the meal.

11:10 a.m.   Lead the group in a song before the PREVENIENT GRACE talk.

1:35 p.m.   Lead the group in a song before the PRIESTHOOD OF ALL BELIEVERS talk.

2:55 p.m.   Lead the group in a song before the JUSTIFYING GRACE talk.

5:20 p.m.   Lead pilgrims in singing "De Colores" as they move from the conference room to dining room. Lead singing of grace before and after dinner.

6:15 p.m.   Conference Room—Lead group in a song before the LIFE OF PIETY talk.

10:15 p.m.   Meditative solo

Saturday

8:00 a.m.   Lead pilgrims in singing "De Colores" on the way from the chapel to the dining room for breakfast. Lead the group in singing grace before and after breakfast.

8:40 a.m.   Conference Room—Lead the group in a song before the GROW THROUGH STUDY talk.

10:00 a.m.   Teach the pilgrims special songs of response for the Saturday Communion service. Lead the group in a song before the MEANS OF GRACE talk.

12:00 noon   Lead everyone in singing grace before and after lunch.

2:55 p.m.   Conference Room—Lead the group in a song before the CHRISTIAN ACTION talk.

4:25 p.m.   Lead the group in a song before the OBSTACLES TO GRACE talk.

5:40 p.m.   Lead singing of grace before and after dinner.

| 6:55 p.m. | Conference Room—Lead group in a song before the DISCIPLESHIP talk. |
| 10:00 p.m. | After the Spiritual Director's explanation of Candlelight, lead the group in singing "Jesus, Jesus" as a round. |

Sunday

6:45 a.m.	Lead Conference Room Team in wake-up music.
8:00 a.m.	Lead group in singing "De Colores" on the way from the chapel to the dining room. Lead singing of grace before and after breakfast.
8:45 a.m.	Lead group in a song before the CHANGING OUR WORLD talk.
9:55 a.m.	Lead group in a song before the SANCTIFYING GRACE talk.
10:55 a.m.	Lead group in a song before the BODY OF CHRIST talk.
12:00 noon	Lead singing of grace before and after lunch.
1:25 p.m.	Lead group in a song before the PERSEVERANCE talk.
2:25 p.m.	Lead group in a song before the FOURTH DAY talk.
4:15 p.m.	Lead group in singing "They Will Know We Are Christians by Our Love" after the pilgrims receive their Emmaus crosses.
5:00 p.m.	If necessary, provide music for the closing Communion service.

SECTION 8—
BOARD
REPRESENTATIVE

At least one member of the Community Board of Directors who is the same gender as the participants serves on the team for each Walk. This person adds to the quality assurance and the maintenance of continuity between each Walk.

Potential board members need to know the possibility that, if elected, they will take a turn serving as a Board Representative for a Walk. If no board member is available to serve in this capacity, a recent past board member familiar with Emmaus ministry models may serve. For a board that plans adequately, these instances will be rare.

The Board Representative keeps a copy of the current version of the *Emmaus Ministries Community Manual* for reference.

RESPONSIBILITIES

Before the Walk

The Board Representative answers questions and gives direction to the Lay Director and Spiritual Director. He or she participates in all team meetings. The Board Representative acts as liaison among the various board committee chairs in delivering information and items for the Walk to the appropriate person.

During the Walk

The Board Representative supports the Lay Director and Conference Room Team, notes difficulties to avoid on future Walks, and discovers improvements for future teams. He or she also serves as adviser on procedure. In the rare circumstance that a Lay and/or Spiritual Director violates the trust of the Board of Directors by steering the Walk in a direction of his or her own choosing, the Board Representative communicates with the Emmaus Board leaders during the Walk as necessary.

The Board Representative is *not* present during the Walk to direct it and does not have a leader's role in the team process unless his or her counsel is sought. The Board Representative functions in a low-key support role among the team members, relating to the team in this capacity through the Lay Director and Spiritual Director. The Board Representative sits at the leaders' table throughout the Walk. The Board Representative does not fill in for other roles on the Walk.

BOARD REPRESENTATIVE'S CHECKLIST

Before the Walk

1. Pray for the Lay Director and Spiritual Director as the team forms.
2. Pray for the team and pilgrims.
3. Obtain a copy of the newest version of the *Emmaus Ministries Community Manual* for use during team formation and the Walk.
4. Obtain any needed materials for the Walk (such as book table instructions, etc.) from the correct board committee chair. Collect suggestions for the book table and pass them on to the correct board committee chair.

During the Walk

1. Come early to the Send-Off to be available to the Lay Director, Spiritual Director, and team.
2. Help introduce pilgrims who seem to be alone to other pilgrims and team members.
3. Sit at the leaders' table.
4. Participate in the Candlelight service as a Conference Room Team member.
5. Help with the chapel service and fellowship time following Candlelight if needed.
6. Help reset the facility after Closing if necessary.
7. When the Spiritual Director asks for corrections on rosters while going through the packet, make changes on one copy to give to the Emmaus Board.

After the Walk

1. Prepare a written report of the Walk.
2. Submit a copy of the report to the Board of Directors, and, if requested, present the report at the next board meeting.
3. Participate in the Fourth Day Follow-Up Meeting with pilgrims and team following the Walk.

Participate in the final team meeting to evaluate the Walk so you can learn from mistakes, celebrate victories, and suggest improvements to the Board of Directors. Coordinate with the Lay Director and Spiritual Director in preparing the evaluation report to submit to the board.

SECTION 9—
TEAM SELECTION
AND TALK
ASSIGNMENTS

The team selection process is not only important to each Walk but also to the health of the entire Emmaus Community. The Team Selection Committee selects all team members except the Lay Director and Spiritual Director and helps make all the talk assignments.

THE TEAM SELECTION COMMITTEE

The Community Board of Directors establishes the Team Selection Committee. The committee consists of a board member (responsible for team selection and serves as committee chair); the Lay and Spiritual Directors; and two to four other members of the Community (nonboard members) representing a cross-section of the Community. All have a broad awareness of the Community membership and a solid understanding of team needs. The Community Spiritual Director works with the Team Selection Committee to provide continuity for the long-range selection of clergy and the cultivation of a pool of future event spiritual leaders.

The Team Selection Committee helps achieve the stated goals for the team selection process:

- **Choosing strong and balanced teams.** The Team Selection Committee provides a broader awareness of prospective team members and their gifts. This awareness helps the team selection process move beyond the limited circle of the team leaders' friends and acquaintances. The committee can more fully consider the experience and gifts of people the team needs.

- **Achieving broad involvement of the Community.** Over time, the Team Selection Committee can strive to involve as many willing members of the Community as possible, for their good and for the health of the Community. An event lay team leader may only have in mind the goal of forming one team for one event; the Team Selection Committee concerns itself with both the building of the team and the building of the entire Community into a body of mature, Christian leaders.

- **Cultivating new leadership.** By following established team selection guidelines, the Team Selection Committee provides continuity in the selection process from event to event. A Team Selection Committee can, therefore, intentionally develop new leaders by encouraging people to move through team roles with increasing leadership over the course of several events.

- **Helping team members grow in grace as servant leaders.** The Team Selection Committee serves as an avenue of corporate discernment for the Community. In this capacity, the Team Selection Committee provides a method of growing Christian leadership in individuals. By involving new leaders, inviting individuals to roles of increasing leadership, and facilitating ongoing conversation about the gifts and graces of everyone, the Team Selection Committee plays an important role in ongoing Christian discipleship.

TEAM SELECTION CHECKLIST

1. After the Team Selection Committee chair has received the confirmed selections of Lay and Spiritual Directors, he or she sets a date with them to meet for team selection (no later than 9 months before the date of the Walk; clergy selection completed 12 months ahead of the Walk).

2. The Team Selection Committee chair notifies committee members of the time and place of the meeting. The Team Selection Committee begins praying for guidance in the team selection process.

3. The Team Selection Committee chair ensures that the Walk team leaders receive The Upper Room and Community-developed materials needed to carry out their roles (such as the *Walk to Emmaus Directors' Manual*, key role checklists, talk outlines, a sample "welcome to the team" letter with team meeting dates, team meeting notes or handouts, etc.).

4. Prior to the team selection meeting, the chair and other committee members gather names of potential team members.

    -   They may obtain names from Community membership records that indicating persons' previous team experience, their active support of previous events (such as the prayer vigil, meal preparation or snack agape, facility setup and cleanup, etc.), and their participation in available training programs.

    -   Community members may submit names of potential team members to the Team Selection Committee throughout the year.

    -   In addition, Walk participants fill out volunteer sheets at the end of their Walk, and the Walk's team members may present names of Walk participants whom they feel would be good team members in the future.

5. The Team Selection Committee should seek a broad representation of the community in coming up with its list of potential team members. The Committee should determine whether persons who previously attended Chrysalis should now be considered adults for the purpose of being selected to team:

    -   Each young person matures at a different rate. The Emmaus community leadership and the Team Selection Committee share the responsibility for determining a young person's readiness to serve as an adult on a Walk team. The key issue is the level of maturity in the young person being considered.

- The decision of when to ask a young person to serve as an adult leader is one to make carefully and prayerfully, based on the characteristics expected of all adult leaders regardless of age. The Team Selection Committee will look for demonstrated leadership skills within their own faith community, the young person's place of employment, and the wider community.

6. For each position on a team, the committee selects a person, with one or two more names as backup. The Lay and Spiritual Directors may come to the meeting prepared to make recommendations to the committee, or they may rely solely on the committee to suggest team members. It is important to emphasize, however, that the selection process is based on prayer and spiritual discernment, not on personal preferences or need for recognition.

7. The Community Spiritual Director works closely with the Walk Spiritual Director in selecting clergy for the teams.

8. After the board approves the Team Selection Committee list(s), the Lay and Spiritual Directors each begin calling their prospective team members. If several prospective team members and their backups cannot serve, then the Lay or Spiritual Director should contact the Team Selection Committee to discuss additional names.

9. When the team has been confirmed, the Lay Director sends the team roster to the Team Selection Committee chairperson and to the communications team for publication.

TEAM SELECTION GUIDELINES

Honoring Emmaus Community Participation

The Team Selection Committee regards participation in an accountable spiritual support group (group reunions or Next Steps groups) and Community Gatherings as a sign of a person's commitment to the Community. While ideally all team members would be active in their specific Walk to Emmaus Reunion Group, Chrysalis Next Steps group, etc., the event lay team leader and a person giving the Fourth Day (Walk to Emmaus) or Next Steps (Chrysalis) talk can only bear authentic witness if they are involved in such a group. Above all, the committee discerns individual gifts for team membership and overall commitment to the aims of Emmaus Ministries.

Anonymous Positions of Servanthood

Emmaus leadership begins and ends with anonymous positions of servanthood, such as participating in the prayer vigil, contributing agape items, or praying in the chapel. This kind of sacrifice and servanthood is the heart of Emmaus Ministries and the place where the development of Christian leadership begins. Those who first give themselves wholeheartedly and joyfully to the humblest duties may eventually be with the participants in the conference room, setting an example and sharing their lives and spirit.

Progressive Servanthood

The design of Emmaus Ministries team structure fosters a progression of responsibility and an increasing level of leadership for everyone. When selecting individuals for team positions, the committee carefully considers each person's leadership experience and the leadership experience of the team. When done well, this process will ensure that all team members build their experience and gain new leadership abilities.

This attitude of progressive servanthood is balanced with the specific gifts and preparedness of an individual to determine where he or she is best suited to serve. An individual who speaks well publicly may be well-suited to speak during the event but may not yet have the organizational abilities to move up to an event team leader position. Such an individual receives the opportunity to develop his or her organizational abilities while also using the gift of speaking. Conversely, an individual who has only served as a music leader but who has speaking or organizational abilities need not be constrained to serving only in a music role. Many positions benefit greatly from specific gifts and abilities, but all individuals may have an opportunity to serve in a progression of responsibilities as they grow.

In the team selection process, the committee keeps in mind that the focus of progressive servanthood is on persons' spiritual formation rather than the position they fill. People can experience great spiritual maturation and never serve on an event team—a great gain to the body of Christ. Conversely, people who serve in multiple roles of increasing responsibility on an event team but move no farther along on their spiritual journey will have missed the more important opportunity. Event leaders pay close attention to their own spiritual journey and empower others to do the same. After all, Emmaus Ministries exists to empower leaders to be the hands and feet of Christ, regardless of the team positions they fill.

The One-Third Rule

A goal of the Team Selection Committee is to staff each team with approximately one-third (1) new conference room team members, (2) second-time or third-time team members, and (3) team veterans. Veterans provide continuity and confidence, while newer members bring fresh energy and enthusiasm. This guideline helps a community integrate fresh faces on the team and expands the Community's leadership base. Each Emmaus event becomes an opportunity to incorporate new persons into teams and to move those with some experience gradually into other leadership positions.

Potential Spiritual Directors and New Clergypersons

The Team Selection Committee strives to include on each team a clergyperson who shows promise as a future event team leader. In this way, those who meet the guidelines to be an event team leader. Spiritual Directors receive regular training and preparation to serve as one by experiencing the entire event from the team side. The Team Selection Committee also tries to include on each team a clergyperson who has never served as a team member. This approach to selection helps the Community expand the pool of potential event clergy team leaders, and deepens clergy appreciation for the Emmaus ministry through their involvement.

The Team Selection Committee plans ahead with the sponsoring organization's spiritual leader and asks clergy twelve months in advance to commit to an entire Emmaus Ministries event. The payoff in clergy support is worth the effort.

Potential Lay Directors

The Team Selection Committee will wisely select at least one assistant lay event team leaders who is experienced and confident in this role and at least one who is new to the job. This choice gives the lay event team leader and team confidence that the assistants' work will be accomplished with competence but also trains new assistants for future teams.

Theological Balance

The Team Selection Committee strives for a sound balance of theological orientations and religious styles on teams. Team members may reflect a diverse set of Christian perspectives, but they must also create an atmosphere of openness and unity for all participants. Teams dominated by any one Christian perspective or denomination do not represent the diversity and unity of the church universal.

Male and Female Clergy on Teams

Team Selection Committees intentionally recruit both men and women clergy among the clergy speakers on teams for both men's and women's events. This rationale represents the reality of pastoral leadership for both men and women in the church universal today. The Office recommends that the Spiritual Director be the same gender as participants.

Grace Talks by Clergy

The concept of grace is the centerpiece of the Emmaus event; the clergy talks provide the background of grace before which the event's message unfolds. These talks are given by those trained by the church in Word and sacrament give these talks to communicate a proper understanding of grace.

Involvement of Many Clergy

An event team has many clergy members, which offers several advantages:

* Many share the workload of the numerous talks and spiritual responsibilities. Each clergy member typically takes time to prepare one talk well and is then free to give attention to the participants.

* Participants hear the message of grace from the perspective and experience of many different clergy.

* More clergy can be involved in the Community and trained more quickly, since not all are required to stay for the entire event. This expands the pool of available and experienced clergy for future teams.

At least two clergy remain in residence for the entire Walk: the Spiritual Director and one Assistant Spiritual Director.

The other assistants present one talk and are encouraged to remain for as much of the event as possible. The Spiritual Director may ask one or more assistants to help with the event's clergy meditations and Communion, and other times as needed.

Lay Table Leaders

Assigning laypersons to the Table Leader roles gives them the opportunity to grow as small-group leaders. Spiritual Directors sometimes inhibit group discussion among laypersons who may view clergy as authorities with all the answers. The largely lay leadership of an event makes a statement to the participants about the commitment, gifts, and leadership potential of church laity.

The leadership makes Table Leader assignments with care. Those chosen have usually been on a team before, preferably as an Assistant Table Leader, or are persons with a proven ability to lead a group. Table Leaders understand Emmaus, listen and empathize, guide discussion, and foster the development of the table families.

THE TEAM ROSTER

Here is a list of the basic assignments on the Conference Room Team.

Lay Director (1)
Spiritual Director (1)
Assistant Spiritual Directors (4)
Assistant Lay Directors (3)
Table Leaders (1 per table)
Assistant Table Leaders (1 per table)
Music Leader (1–3, same gender; if 3, one must be new to the position)
Board Representative (1)

Given thirty-six pilgrims and six tables, the number of team members is twenty-two or twenty-three. The fifteen talks are assigned to these Conference Room Team members only:

PRIORITY (Assistant Lay Director)
PREVENIENT GRACE (Assistant Spiritual Director)
PRIESTHOOD OF ALL BELIEVERS (Table Leader or Assistant Table Leader)
JUSTIFYING GRACE (Assistant Spiritual Director)
LIFE OF PIETY (Table Leader or Assistant Table leader)
GROW THROUGH STUDY (Table Leader or Assistant Table Leader)
MEANS OF GRACE (Lead or head Spiritual Director for the weekend)
CHRISTIAN ACTION (Table Leader or Assistant Table Leader)
OBSTACLES TO GRACE (Assistant Spiritual Director)
DISCIPLESHIP (Table Leader or Assistant Table Leader)

CHANGING OUR WORLD (Table Leader or Assistant Table Leader)
SANCTIFYING GRACE (Assistant Spiritual Director)
BODY OF CHRIST (Table Leader or Assistant Table Leader)
PERSEVERANCE (Lay Director)
FOURTH DAY (Assistant Lay Director)

TALK ASSIGNMENTS

Length of Talks

Throughout the Walk, various team members present fifteen talks to the pilgrims. All the talks work together to present a unified message. Except for the MEANS OF GRACE talk, no talk exceeds twenty-five minutes. Adhering to this time limit for talks displays God's equal provision for all, facilitates the pilgrims' experience, and does not single out one speaker with a longer talk. Beyond twenty-five minutes, pilgrims will become restless, lack concentration, and lose interest. At that point, table discussion becomes exceedingly difficult. Speakers who exceed the time recommendation disrupt the schedule and place stress on the Lay Director to recapture the lost time.

Preselected Assignments

PERSEVERANCE Talk by the Lay Director

Emmaus makes the Lay Director responsible for presenting the talk on PERSEVERANCE. This assignment exists for two reasons.

First, by the end of the Walk, the Lay Director represents to the pilgrims the commitment, sacrifice, and perseverance that characterize the whole team and to which the pilgrims are being called as Christians. Though the pilgrims may weary of listening to talks by Sunday afternoon, they remain open to a word from the Lay Director—a special person who has now earned the right to speak and be heard. At that point in a long Walk, the Lay Director's unexpected appearance as a speaker may move the pilgrims who understand this to be a person who has sacrificed and persevered as a leader.

Second, the Lay Director represents one who possesses spiritual maturity and embodies the Emmaus method for living described in the PERSEVERANCE talk. This talk gives the Lay Director an opportunity to pull together the message of the Walk and say what still needs to be said about living in the Fourth Day, to explain and bear personal witness to the value of the group reunion as a means of persevering in grace for the rest of life.

MEANS OF GRACE Talk/Dying Moments Communion by the Spiritual Director

Emmaus assigns to the Weekend Spiritual Director the responsibility of presenting the MEANS OF GRACE talk and conducting the Dying Moments Communion service that follows. The assignment of these responsibilities falls to the Spiritual Director for the following reasons.

First, this assignment provides assurance that a known and trusted clergyperson will handle these critical moments during the Walk. This person has been with the pilgrims from the start of the Walk and will be present through its end.

Second, this assignment assures the Board of Directors that the MEANS OF GRACE talk and the Dying Moments Communion will be given by clergy with the experience and ability to handle these responsibilities with grace and clarity. The Spiritual Director may request assistance for the Dying Moments Communion from another clergyperson who is staying through the entire Walk.

PRIORITY Talk by an Assistant Lay Director

An experienced Assistant Lay Director gives the talk on PRIORITY. This assignment keeps a Table Leader from being absent from the table for the first talk and discussion and allows every table to get off to a good start. This decision assures that a seasoned team member will give the first talk of the weekend and properly launch the Walk. The theme of PRIORITY underlies the entire Walk.

FOURTH DAY Talk by an Assistant Lay Director

An experienced Assistant Lay Director gives the talk titled FOURTH DAY. As with the first talk, PRIORITY, this allows all team members to be at their tables to facilitate the transition to the personal events that follow this talk.

Progression of Talk Assignments

The progression of talk assignments for team members varies from community to community. Some communities follow a specific order, slowly moving both lay and clergy team members through the talks occurring early in the event to those occurring near the end of the event. Other communities only consider the number and variety of talks a team member has given. Still others reserve particular lay talks for the most experienced Emmaus Ministries team members.

The committee assigns team members topics that they can communicate with insight and experience whether they are new or seasoned team members.

SECTION 10— GENERAL INSTRUCTIONS FOR THE TEAM

TEAM PREPARATION

All Conference Room Team members familiarize themselves with The Walk to Emmaus by reading these instructions, especially the pages giving key points of the talks and the general points to make in discussions after the talks (in the "Team Formation through Team Meetings" section). This will help you lead your table group in discussing each talk. Speakers preview their talks before the weekend.

BEFORE THE WALK

Team members arrive at the Walk site before the pilgrims so that any team meeting or team commissioning service occurs before the pilgrims' arrival. Mix with the pilgrims as they arrive. Avoid talking too much with other team members; concentrate your efforts on the pilgrims; do not show too much affection at the beginning.

THURSDAY NIGHT AND FIRST DAY

The three days have distinct phases. Thursday night is the spiritual retreat, a meditative time intended to make the pilgrims receptive to the message of Emmaus.

On Thursday night, final selection will be made for table assignments. At the evening meeting, team members finalize preparation for the Walk and report on the progress of the pilgrims.

On Friday, the talks focus on living in grace. This day centers on God and the grace God offers.

Reminders for Table Leaders and Assistant Table Leaders

* Encourage participation from each person at the table.
* Avoid overreacting to statements—both yourself and other pilgrims. Pay attention to the progression of ideas expressed by the pilgrims; report any serious problems to the Spiritual Director.
* Take extensive notes as an example to the pilgrims.

- Anticipate and encourage the pilgrims to give everything they can by your good example in all you do.
- Be careful not to dominate.
- Listen, listen; love, love.

Reminders for Other Team Members
- Spread out among the pilgrims during chapel visits and mealtimes and mingle with the pilgrims.
- Return to the table (the speaker) *after* the discussion and summary representation (poster, skit, song, etc.) of the talk.
- Exemplify the qualities of true piety—authenticity, courage, and joy.

SECOND DAY

On Saturday, the talks shift their attention to Christ and strive to teach pilgrims how to be apostles or leaders for Christ. Beginning to know Christ intimately is the theme.

The message of Emmaus may stir deep feelings in pilgrims. Stay open to deeper sharing with them but don't force it. Affirm their responses to the Walk thus far.

THIRD DAY

The talks on Sunday emphasize what Christian community looks like in action. Attention focuses on the Holy Spirit. By this time, an enthusiastic spirit generally prevails.

The pilgrims will begin thinking about their return home. Try to keep their minds on living for the moment and not anticipating.

Closing Ceremony

This ceremony serves as a summation of the three days. Team members stress the value of continued fellowship with other Christians (through accountability groups and Emmaus Gatherings), working at future events, prayers and sacrifices, and attendance at future Candlelights and Closings.

Fourth Day Follow-Up Meeting

Each team member can encourage and facilitate efforts to assist the pilgrims from their table in joining an accountability group and attending Emmaus Gatherings. Coordinate these efforts with the pilgrims' sponsors.

GENERAL REMARKS

The Emmaus community is not a closed society but a movement within Christianity.

The team devotes the entire Walk to their new brothers and sisters in Christ. The following proverb expresses the team's approach:

Pray as if everything depended on Christ;
work as if everything depended on you.

SECTION 11—
THE SPIRIT OF EMMAUS

The spirit in which an Emmaus ministry event is conducted is none other than the Holy Spirit.

In Galatians 5:22-26, the apostle Paul lists "the fruit of the Spirit," characteristics of the Holy Spirit manifested in people's attitudes and behavior. This fruit represents the character of a team properly formed in the spirit of Jesus Christ. We want participants to feast on this fruit throughout their event. The fruit of the Spirit serves as a good backdrop for describing team attitudes and practices. Team leaders can cultivate among team members a readiness to embrace the quality of community life that the Holy Spirit brings by reviewing one aspect of the fruit of the Spirit at each team meeting.

LOVE

An atmosphere of hospitality and acceptance characterizes the weekend community. The team promotes the feeling of an open and opportune space for pilgrims to respond freely and honestly to the gospel of grace in the presence of people who care, a time in which the pilgrims can rediscover themselves in relationship with God. The environment of unconditional love allows people to lower their defenses and allow God to touch their lives with grace. The team motto for Kairos (the prison expression of Cursillo) suits Emmaus equally well: "Listen, listen, love, love."

However, this love draws attention to God—not to team members. An ancient image depicts the spiritual life as a wagon wheel with spokes connecting at the center. The center represents God in Jesus Christ, and the wheel rim represents people. As we turn and move toward the center, we, at the same time, draw closer to one another. When we attempt to move closer to one another along the rim of human need and natural inclination, we do not necessarily move closer to God. Nor do we necessarily move closer to lasting, spiritual relationships with one another. Emmaus attempts to turn people's attention toward God and draw them closer to God. This process then draws participants together as spiritual friends into a Christian community of the Holy Spirit's making.

The wagon wheel image of the spiritual life reminds the team members that their behavior calls attention to God, not to themselves. The image also reminds the team that God's presence does not result from human togetherness or a feeling of human closeness. Team members need not take action that they believe will accelerate feelings of intimacy or push pilgrims to share beyond their levels of willingness. God will draw the pilgrims together as they turn their attention to God's welcoming love and as their hearts overflow with the gift of that love in the company of one another. On the Walk, pilgrims will experience how the grace of God in Jesus Christ draws people together into a new community of the Holy Spirit's own creation, a community centered in the freedom of God's love rather than in the egoism and neediness intrinsic to human love.

JOY

A Walk has many occasions of true joy: the joy of singing, the joy of self-expression or uninhibited laughter, the joy of insight, the joy of liberation from the shackles of sin or inner hurt or murderous anger, the joy of knowing God's presence, the joy of feeling accepted, and the joy of giving one's life wholeheartedly and without reservation to Jesus Christ. The joy of Emmaus comes in moments of seriousness and in moments of great fun. In these ways, team members, as well as pilgrims, experience the joy of the Lord and of life together in Christian community. They let their joy be known in song, sharing, and enthusiasm for the Christian ideal. The team can set the tone for the Walk through an attitude of joyful anticipation of the Lord's coming to each person in some real, though unforeseen, way along the road.

The team takes care that the expression of joy in fun does not give way to boisterousness and getting carried away: allowing jokes to get out of hand or letting people go too far in making fun of one another. Extroverts—pilgrims or team members—can take over the weekend in such a way that introverts feel left out and do not participate. During the fun time of sharing summaries and the various representations in the evenings, laughter and hilarity may totally overshadow and render pointless the recap of the day's talks and the sharing of each table's insights. The team and pilgrims can have fun while also showing appreciation and sensitivity toward the thoughts and creativity expressed at each table.

Getting carried away also occurs when negative traditions such as "stealing the bell" and the amusement this creates for a few disrupts weekends for all. Stealing the bell is a tradition among team members who feel a need to make the Walk livelier. Team members' attempts to create more fun result from insecurity about the adequacy of the Walk, a desire to make sure the pilgrims have the experience they themselves had on their Walk, or perhaps boredom and a need to make the Walks more exciting for themselves. Team members, especially team leaders, remain aware of the team's influence on the atmosphere of the Walk and share concerns in the nightly team meetings.

PEACE

People who walk in the Spirit enjoy the fruit of peace with God and one another. Team members exhibit conscious care for their relationship with God and other people and practice the peace that comes from faith in God's love and direction. Then team members enjoy the inner security of being only themselves on Walks. They need not act more spiritual than usual, more religious than others, or make a perfect report on their Christian life and home. However, team members actively strive to practice their piety, study, and action and want to live an authentic Christian life. Team members who feel they must work to maintain an image or who pretend to uphold a way of life that they have never practiced will find no peace.

Peace also comes from faith in God's love for all people. Participants in Emmaus come from many denominations, races, and walks of life. They may differ considerably in their views on doctrine, church, politics, and the world. They find themselves at different levels of Christian maturity and experience. Yet, despite their differences, team members share the peace of Christ with the pilgrims and foster community among them by modeling Christian tolerance and charity toward all.

Christian tolerance does not imply indifference toward sound Christian belief and theology. It does mean focusing on the common essentials of Christian faith while not letting differences over doctrine become more powerful than the love of Christ in relationships. The team's attitude is as follows: If your heart is as my heart, then give me your hand. (See 2 Kings 10:15.) Emmaus attempts to set forth the essentials of Christian faith and practice that characterize the mainstream of Christian tradition, the gift of God's peace indeed "surpasses all understanding" (Phil. 4:7).

Team members do not set the pilgrims straight on details of doctrine. Rather, they "love, love; listen, listen," leaving the rest to God and trusting the process of the weekend. When differences over belief arise among pilgrims, team members challenge them to affirm the gift in each other's perspectives, to explore those beliefs more fully with their pastors when they return home, and to stay focused on the message and experience of the Walk.

Team members are always the first to extend the hand of Christian fellowship. "Let peace begin with me" becomes their personal motto and prayer. The team can foster the peace of Christ among the pilgrims by modeling an open and nondefensive spirit, by speaking the truth in love, and by being quick to forgive or say "I'm sorry." The team members keep in mind that they have been given the peace of Christ so they can pass that peace to others. This peace comes from a vital relationship with God.

PATIENCE

A Walk is a full but slow walk with the Lord. Even though the pilgrims follow the same path, each experience is unique. The pilgrims hear and see the Lord in their own way, according to their needs and God's will for them at the time of the Walk. Team members guard against the temptation to run ahead of the pilgrims, to hurry them toward their meaningful moment along the way or to rob them of their own experience by previewing upcoming scenes: "Wait until you see what's going to happen next!"

Working on a team requires patience—not only with the pilgrims but also with the work of the Lord in the process. A definition of functional atheism is the belief operative in people who profess God but whose lifestyle reflects an assumption that nothing will happen unless they make it happen themselves. Team members are functional atheists when they try to do

God's work for God, try to speed up the movement of the Holy Spirit, try to "save" the pilgrims or bring them to a "decision" or manipulate an emotionally charged atmosphere. God transforms the pilgrims; team members simply love them, openly share their own faith stories and witness, and give the pilgrims space to explore their relationship with God among people who care and listen.

One pilgrim bore witness to the power of patience on the part of the team. After what was for him a life-changing event, he remarked, "What really surprised me was that the team members at my table were not putting anything over on me. They didn't make me feel I was bad or wrong because I didn't see things their way or have an experience with God like theirs. I felt free to respond honestly the whole time, and I did. About midway I was overcome by the enormous love behind the whole weekend and what was for me an experience of God. I can't believe I'm saying this, but for the first time in my life I think I know what it means to say I know Jesus."

The patience of this pilgrim's Table Leaders and team leaders gave him freedom to experience the Walk in his own way. They trusted the process. Team members can trust the Holy Spirit to touch the pilgrims' lives through the scheduled activities and interactions of the Walk in ways that may or may not be outwardly evident.

Sometimes team members, more than the pilgrims, need not anticipate. Leadership also stresses that team members expect no formulaic response from the pilgrims, that each person's response to the Walk will be individual. While true in theory, individual response is not true in practice unless team members let go of their expectations for the Walk and replace them with a prayer of thanksgiving for God's grace already at work in each pilgrim's life. They open the way by giving themselves as open and caring instruments for the fulfillment of God's purpose in God's own time in each pilgrim's life.

Team members display patience when they allow the pilgrims to have their own experience and honor the different places pilgrims find themselves on their spiritual journeys. Team members show patience when they relinquish the presumption of knowing what the pilgrims really need and trust God to touch each one in a unique way. Team members exhibit patience when their manner communicates respect for the pilgrims' spiritual integrity, thus making the Walk an accepting space where they feel free to respond authentically to God's presence. Team members employ patience when they trust the process of Emmaus and the sovereign power of grace in people's lives.

KINDNESS

Kindness is love expressed in specific acts of caring, attention, and undeserved charity. The pilgrims experience the kindness of God through the attention of the team and the Emmaus community to the pilgrims' every need and the extraordinarily detailed care that make Emmaus a special gift. Saint Augustine once wrote, "[God,] you are good and all-powerful, caring for each one of us as though the only one in your care." This is the kind of love we hope the pilgrims will experience through the kindness of the team and Community. A pilgrim, a

United Methodist district superintendent, once described his experience of a Walk as "three days of Christian affirmation."

Team members set out to acknowledge, converse with, involve, affirm, serve, and pray for the pilgrims so that they may know their value as persons and as citizens of God's reign. Another pilgrim noted, "In every phase of my life, I am in charge. I am constantly giving. One of the hardest things on the Walk for me was letting someone else be in charge and allowing myself to learn again to receive, not only from people but from God." Emmaus frees the pilgrims from their need to control so they can receive and experience the grace of God's love for who they are, rather than for what or how much they can do.

Emmaus is an extraordinary act of God's kindness. Few programs involve the investment of so much from so many for the sake of so few. Team members take care that kindness does not turn into control. Pilgrims do not experience God's kindness when the team's attention becomes smothering watchfulness. While the communal and scheduled nature of Emmaus requires that the team leaders do the best they can to keep the pilgrims on the evenly paced schedule, they do this with kindness, sensitivity, and respect.

Team and Community helpers do not call attention to their acts of kindness, even in the Closing. The Lay Director may recognize the persons who have contributed to the weekend in order to give the pilgrims the opportunity to express their gratitude. However, it is contrary to the spirit of Emmaus for the Lay or Spiritual Director to pour enormous praise upon the team and Community helpers or single out specific members for applause. The Closing's focus remains on the pilgrims and God's work in their lives.

Pilgrims are <u>always</u> treated with kindness and respect.

GOODNESS

A fruit of being grafted to the true vine of Jesus Christ is the goodness of God's self-giving and sacrificial love. Jesus said, "No one is good but God alone" (Mark 10:18). Jesus embodied the fullness of God's goodness in selfless love and humble servanthood.

"Let the same mind be in you that was in Christ Jesus, who, though he was in the form of God, did not regard equality with God as something to be exploited, but emptied himself, taking the form of a slave, being born in human likeness. And being found in human form, he humbled himself and became obedient to the point of death—even death on a cross" (Phil. 2:5-8).

Jesus, through his sacrificial love, gave up his advantage *over* human beings to become an advantage *to* them; he surrendered his divine credentials to live without distinction as a human among humans, thereby bringing God's grace to them. Jesus, as a humble servant, called attention to God not himself. He accomplished what he did under authority, not of his own accord. He did not belong to himself; he was the healing hands and saving Word of God. His success was God's success; he found his reward in God's glory.

The team and Emmaus community are to manifest the same spirit of selfless love and humble servanthood. In fact, team members and the Community understand their responsibilities for the Walk as spiritual exercises in selfless love and Christian servanthood. Team members' own need for affirmation and attention, while real, is cared for during the weekly team meeting prior to the Walk and during the nightly team meetings during the Walk. Team members need to be free to serve the pilgrims during the weekend without their egos getting in the way.

Egos can become stumbling blocks along the way when team members find themselves calling attention to their own or each other's giftedness or sacrificial goodness or acting out of a personal need for recognition. Egos become stumbling blocks whenever team members make themselves the center of attention with their humor, their presumption of authority, or by displaying their gifts, rather than using their gifts to turn the pilgrims' attention to Jesus Christ and to building the community.

Egos become stumbling blocks whenever team members talk more than they listen and speak for their table family in the evenings instead of putting the pilgrims forward. Stumbling blocks crop up whenever the pilgrims are led to applaud each speaker after talks, thus calling attention to the person and the needs of the speaker instead of the message the speaker presented; or when team members make a public show of affirming a speaker as he or she leaves the conference room, instead of reserving their accolades for the Prayer Chapel or another time. Whenever speakers make their talks occasions for excessive emotional display or disproportionate amounts of personal witness, thus calling attention primarily to their own experiences and not to the message of their talk, egos have become stumbling blocks.

When team leaders who present general agape overstate how much everyone is sacrificing for the pilgrims, thus making them feel they ought to feel gratitude toward the Emmaus community rather than letting the agape elicit gratitude and love as a free response, or when persons in support roles allow their personal needs for affirmation or recognition become an issue during a Walk and a point of concern for the team, egos have become stumbling blocks. Egos get in the way when Community members begin to see support functions in the background of the Walk as less important and less desirable avenues of service than visible participation on the Conference Room Team. Those who serve in support roles do represent the invisible backdrop of prayer, sacrificial love, and anonymous servanthood that reflects the Walk's power in the love of God. No one is beyond the need or the privilege of these forms of servanthood, no matter how many times they have served as Lay Director or Spiritual Director or team members.

Practices that highlight distinctions between pilgrims and team members can also become potential instruments of egoism and barriers to Christian community. This barrier arises when teams present any aspects of a Walk or Emmaus itself as a gift from the team to the pilgrims. In this way, the team proudly makes itself the selfless giver of good things and the focus of the pilgrims' gratitude for the weekend. The team's sacrifice always becomes self-evident in time without the team's calling attention to it. Furthermore, Emmaus is not a gift of the team but of the risen Christ who walks with pilgrims and gives them the Holy Spirit through the church and the Emmaus community. Though the team members have responsibilities as companions who have walked this road before, they are still humble pilgrims on the journey to God and receive grace from the Walk no less than those who are walking to Emmaus for the first time.

Here are some Emmaus team guidelines and procedures that will help the team members indicate their unity with the participants:

Team members remain quiet and low-key about their team status and about their past participation and leadership in Emmaus, for all the reasons stated above. Team members do not keep their identity a secret nor do they attempt to infiltrate the pilgrims with undercover team members. The pilgrims see the entire team on Thursday evening when the Lay Director asks the team to stand in the introductory presentation to Emmaus. Remaining low-key about team identity simply emphasizes their commonality with the pilgrims; they serve humbly and avoid the barrier to community that an attitude of status can present.

- **After the Thursday evening introduction of the team and the Friday morning table assignments,** Assistant Table Leaders serve in anonymity. Few pilgrims remember the persons recognized as team members the previous evening, and it presents no problem if they do. The Assistant Table Leader's role is an exercise in solidarity with the pilgrims, selfless servanthood, and low-key support for the Table Leader and the pilgrims' participation. The persons in this role never make a game of their identity or carry it to the point of deception. Deliberately misleading the pilgrims plants seeds of suspicion and distrust and works against the purpose of the guideline: development of community on the Walk. Assistant Table Leaders relate to the participants as pilgrims without special status and set an example for wholehearted table participation.

- **Team members are housed in the same facilities** and rooms with the pilgrims, except for the Assistant Lay Directors, Lay Director, Spiritual Director, Music Leaders and Board Representative. Many fruitful conversations occur in the rooms between pilgrims and team members when housed together. No functional reason exists to separate team members from the pilgrims, except for the small inconvenience of returning to the rooms late after the evening team meetings. The only other motives for segregating the team from the pilgrims revolve around privilege and extra convenience that may come from separate quarters, neither of which is congruent with the servant role of the team and the spirit of Emmaus.

- **Team members do not wear their Emmaus crosses or any special Emmaus clothing** that distinguishes them as team members or as veterans of Emmaus until the commissioning, Closing, and Fourth Day activities. Team members and pilgrims alike begin again and again on the path of Christ. Humility marks the veteran on the spiritual journey—not crosses or clothing that signify the privilege of a few on a Walk.

Emmaus has no place for personal or team glorification. Every part of the method and the manner of Emmaus puts Jesus Christ at the center, calls attention to Christ's goodness and not the team's, and fosters Christian community among all as pilgrims on the Walk.

FAITHFULNESS

Each Walk depends on the team members' faithfulness to God, to team leaders, to The Upper Room Emmaus model, and to the pilgrims. When persons accept the call to serve on an Emmaus team, they enter an implicit covenant with God and the Emmaus community to make the best Walk possible for the people who participate. This covenant involves an agreement to serve under the direction of the appointed Lay and Spiritual Directors of the team and to support their leadership wholeheartedly during team formation and during the Walk. It also involves an agreement by team leaders and members to abide faithfully by the purpose and procedures of The Upper Room Emmaus Ministries.

Team members keep faith with one another by attending team meetings, praying for one another during team formation, and helping one another prepare for talks or other responsibilities. The team keeps faith with the Lay and Spiritual Directors by respecting their personal and team schedules, being prepared for assignments at team meetings, praying for their strength and wisdom to lead, honoring their authority, and being their friend throughout.

Team members, leaders, and the Board of Directors keep faith with The Upper Room Emmaus Ministries and the Emmaus movement by following the Emmaus manuals and outlines—a responsibility particularly incumbent upon the Lay and Spiritual Directors of each Walk. This commitment to the program's intent assures the quality of the Emmaus experience being offered and its continuity with Emmaus across the rest of the movement as a trusted instrument of Christian renewal. The manuals represent the objective standards and procedures for Emmaus, the common ground upon which a team can grow in a shared understanding of what Emmaus is and how to conduct it properly.

Team members also keep faith with the pilgrims—first through fidelity to the aims of The Upper Room Emmaus Ministries, second by being a true spiritual friend. We all need people who see Christ in us. Team members help the pilgrims claim the promise in their lives, affirm their gifts. They support the pilgrims' desire to live their lives to the fullest in grace. Team members keep faith by holding confidences as well. Finally, team members keep faith with the pilgrims *after* the weekend by following up on friendships that developed during the Walk, keeping them in prayer, writing to them, helping pilgrims develop accountability groups and participate in church, and showing them in every way possible that their Walk experience was real.

GENTLENESS

The highly-structured nature of a Walk requires gentleness from its leadership. A regimented approach to the Walk is antithetical to the spirit of Emmaus. A Walk is a long and renewing stroll not a forced march. Team members exercise discipline in their leadership, but the motivation for the discipline is care for the pilgrims' ultimate experience during the Walk. Though leaders want to enlist the complete participation of every pilgrim on every step of the journey, they need not be overbearing or controlling; it is a matter of attitude and style. A commanding or belittling style *works against* the pilgrims' desire to cooperate and only demonstrates that team members have not appropriated the grace they talk about. A gentle and respectful approach *works with* the pilgrims' desire to cooperate and their freedom to be there. Such an approach communicates care for persons and for the program and conveys the grace of the Lord's companionship on the Walk.

Persons exercising gentleness in leadership conduct the Walk with firmness and flexibility. The team is both firm and confident with the pilgrims about the value of each part of the Emmaus experience and the kind of participation being asked of them. The team members also respond with flexibility when needed. Even if the entire Walk is technically flawless, the experience will fall short of being a means of grace to pilgrims who experience the team as rigid to the point of insensitivity to people. Jesus taught his disciples about the kind of leadership Emmaus calls for. It is the only kind of leadership Christians are given authority to exercise in Jesus' name.

> Jesus called them to him and said, "You know that the rulers of the Gentiles lord it over them, and their great ones are tyrants over them. It will not be so among you; but whoever wishes to be great among you must be your servant, and whoever wishes to be first among you must be your slave; just as the Son of Man came not to be served but to serve, and to give his life as a ransom for many."
>
> —Matthew 20:25-28

Jesus modeled and motivated a leadership style based on the power of love rather than position. Team members and leaders win the pilgrims' respect through spiritual authenticity and willingness to go out of their way for other people's good. Moreover, Lay and Spiritual Directors will model this kind of leadership during team formation if they desire the same from the team on the Walk. Jesus taught the disciples through example more than words and passed on to them the spirit of his gentle style among people. Team leaders do likewise with team members, leading them with love as well as discipline, affirmation as well as expectation, and committing to help them give their best on the Walk.

SELF-CONTROL

Christians practice self-control by allowing the love of Christ to rule them (2 Cor. 5:14), beginning with the tongue. Team members guard against the temptation to talk rather than listen, to dominate discussions, or to presume the role of a spiritual guru who can tell the pilgrims what they "really need." Team members also avoid the temptation to send coded messages to one another that the pilgrims cannot understand or to make public references to inside jokes that leave the pilgrims feeling like outsiders. James's words are so true: "The tongue is a small member, yet it boasts of great exploits" (James 3:5). Team members avoid letting their team membership become a source and/or a platform for spiritual pride. Having previously attended an Emmaus event does not imply more maturity in Christ than pilgrims just starting out.

Team members also allow the love of Christ to control their moral and spiritual judgments of the pilgrims. Persons of goodwill and sincere Christian faith differ in their stance (how they discern God's will) on significant moral issues of the day, ranging from drinking and abortion to nuclear weapons and the best ways to care for society's poor. Team members acknowledge this reality and honor other moral positions, even if they disagree with them. They never presume to represent *the* Christian position on difficult issues of the day, and they help pilgrims listen to persons who hold an alternate perspective.

Moreover, team members allow the love of Christ to temper the age-old tendency in pharisaism. Pharisees require that people's religious lives pass the Pharisees' own spiritual litmus test and conform to their rules for salvation. Pharisees tend to assume that unless people have taken on their particular brand of religious experience or practice, they are not whole. Yet not everyone attending a Walk needs a born-again experience, baptism in the Holy Spirit, commitment to a particular kind of missional concern, special healing, or contemplative prayer experience. Furthermore, Emmaus is not the arena in which to promote personal religious experience and emphasis. These "accents" meet needs and may be central to some groups' experiences, but none represents the whole gospel as conveyed by the mainstream of Christian tradition. None alone is necessary for grace, salvation, or a vital Christian life. Team members do the pilgrims and the Emmaus movement a favor by controlling their desire to impose their religious agendas on the Walk, over and above the aims of Emmaus itself.

Pilgrims are at different places on their spiritual journeys and will receive the grace they need on the Walk in different ways. For one person, the Walk is a new and life-altering experience of God's love; for another, the Walk is an enjoyable reinforcement of an already rich faith and practice. For one pilgrim, Emmaus becomes an experience of liberation from an old hurt or hate; for another, it provides an occasion to reorder priorities or make a commitment to a life of service. For still another pilgrim, the Walk is sufficient as a learning experience in Christian theology; for still another, it means making some new and close friends. The road to Emmaus begins wherever people are when they are called to participate and ends in the fellowship of friends breaking bread together in communion with the Lord. The only rule of the road is the love of Christ.

SECTION 12— TEAM FORMATION THROUGH TEAM MEETINGS

ORIENTATION BEFORE TEAM FORMATION

The Emmaus Board of Directors has responsibility for organizing and presenting an orientation session for all Conference Room Team members and support committee members before the first team meeting. Board members who are not serving during the upcoming Walks conduct the orientation session. If the board holds the orientation session prior to a pair of Walks (a Men's Walk and a Women's Walk), the orientation session can include all individuals who will serve on the upcoming pair of Walks. Here are the objectives of the orientation session:

- Describe the roles and responsibilities of each team member and behind-the-scenes support personnel.

- Explain the need for a cloistered environment for the conference room, and emphasize that support committee members must not intrude into this cloistered environment.

- Remind support committee members of their role of anonymous servanthood. Encourage them to encircle the cloistered conference room with prayer and to become a Christian community of support for the conference room group.

REASONS FOR TEAM FORMATION

The team-formation process requires twenty-three to twenty-six hours of team meetings. An intentional team-formation process is essential to fulfilling the goals of the Emmaus movement for five reasons:

1. To prepare the team members functionally.
2. To prepare team members spiritually.
3. To build a spirit of Christian community.
4. To train future leaders for Emmaus.
5. To develop Christian leaders for work outside the Community. (For a complete description of the above five reasons, see the "Teams" section of the *Emmaus Ministries Community Manual.*)

PARTICIPATION IN TEAM MEETINGS

It is essential that team members participate in the entire team process. Those contacting prospective team members tell them of the expected commitment. In many communities, a general rule of thumb is that team members participate in at least three-fourths of the total number of team meetings.

Clergy team members are expected to participate in team meetings as well. The Spiritual Director sets the example by committing to attend all team meetings and previewing the talks. The two clergypersons who will remain in residence during the entire Walk attend all the team meetings. All clergy are expected to be present for the preview of the other clergy members' talks and try to participate in every team meeting.

Team meetings involve only the Conference Room Team: Those who will be in the conference room with the participants for the entire event. Though support persons working behind the scenes are an integral part of the Walk, team meeting attendance will not directly help them perform their duties. Involving support persons in team meetings may unnecessarily overextend these servants, which may prevent them from making fuller commitments in the future. Communities must guard against this danger. Emmaus does not serve its purpose well if it ties up so many Community members in team preparation and Walks that they neglect their regular Fourth Day responsibilities (church, family, or community) or if the Emmaus community experiences burn out between Walks.

AGENDA FOR A TEAM MEETING

Team meetings generally consist of several elements:

- **Worshiping together** at the beginning of each meeting. Lay and clergy team members can rotate leadership for this time of worship or Communion.

- **Sharing our spiritual lives** in "floating" group reunions. For a few minutes after worship, the event team leader (Lay Director) may invite participants to gather in groups of two or three to respond to a question or two from the group reunion card or other questions the Lay Director chooses. This sharing fosters team relationships, focuses the team on the spiritual life, and readies the team inwardly for the remainder of the meeting.

- **Developing a thorough understanding of Emmaus.** For a few minutes at each meeting, the Lay or Spiritual Director expands team members' understanding of the ministry by reviewing one aspect of the program and the team's responsibilities.

- **Helping one another prepare** for and practice the tasks: talk previews, table leadership, and music leadership.

- **Praying together** at the close of the meeting and throughout team formation. Prayer undergirds and empowers each event from beginning to end, including the prayers of the team throughout team formation.

Team meetings are not the place for working out details of what happens behind the scenes. These responsibilities belong to specific persons who work outside of team meetings. Good planning and wise use of team meeting time fosters positive team morale and confidence in the team leaders.

PREVIEWING TALKS

All speakers—lay and clergy alike—present their talk to the team just as they will present the talk at the event. This gives the speakers the chance to practice the talk and gain strength from the team's affirmation and suggestions for improvements. No one is above improvement, and the team offers suggestions in an atmosphere of care and affirmation. Previewing the talks underscores the fact that each speaker depends upon the others to convey the total message of the event. When a team member presents a talk and receives the team's comments, the talk no longer belongs just to that speaker but to the entire team. No speaker surprises the team on the Walk with a radically different talk than the one previewed without consulting the Lay Director and/or Spiritual Director. A person who refuses to share his or her talk with the team before the Walk chooses not to be a team member.

Before each speaker previews his or her talk, the Lay Director asks the speaker's team prayer partner or another team member to pray aloud for the speaker. The group, under the leadership of the Music Director, sings the appropriate traditional song as determined by the Board of Directors (such as "Sing Hallelujah"). Then the Assistant Lay Director makes the "With a clean sheet of paper. . . ." introduction, and the speaker leads the group in the Prayer to the Holy Spirit. The speaker then introduces the talk; writes the title of the talk and his or her name on the board, displays a piece of poster board with the title written on it, or has someone project a visual on a screen; presents the talk using any planned visual aids; concludes the talk by saying "Amen" or "De Colores" and leaves the room. For the PRIORITY talk, the speaker does not use the Prayer to the Holy Spirit and does not end the talk with "Amen" or "De Colores." Each speaker prepares to present the finished talk before the team just as though presenting on the Walk.

Team members review the talk by listening for the main points of the talk outline, considering the speaker's success at bringing fundamental points to life with illustration or personal witness, and noting any obstacles to communication in the speaker's content or style. The Lay Director gives team members copies of "Key Points of Talks" listed below or from the *Walk to Emmaus Team Manual* to aid in evaluation. To maintain consistent quality and content of each Walk, each speaker needs to cover the main points of his or her talk.

When the speaker finishes and leaves the room for the prayer chapel, the Lay Director forms simulated table groups and asks the team members to review the talk by reflecting upon at least these two questions:

1. What about this talk can you affirm?
2. How can this talk still be improved?

The team receives a few moments of silence to reflect upon the talk considering these questions and then members share their reflections in the small groups. Table Leaders take turns leading the group discussion, commenting on the first question before moving to the second. After ten minutes of discussion, the Lay Director calls the speaker back into the room to receive from each Table Leader the affirmations and suggestions for improvement. Once a statement or suggestion has surfaced, groups do not need to repeat it. Following the table reports, the Lay Director opens the floor for other comments and clarifications.

The talk preview affords an indispensable opportunity for team members to learn to speak the truth in love with one another. The Lay and Spiritual Directors foster an atmosphere of caring and affirmation that cuts off insensitive and unnecessary criticism while challenging each speaker with the truth about needed improvements. The Spiritual Director actively participates in talk previews to ensure theological soundness, clarity, and relevance to life and stands ready to meet with team members who face difficulties pulling their talks together. As a good general rule, two-thirds of the talk will come from the outline and one-third will be the speaker's original insights and illustrations.

KEY POINTS OF TALKS

PRIORITY: Some basic differences distinguish humans from the rest of created order. Humans can set priorities and thus choose an ideal, informed by reason, for their life.

- The created order—three kingdoms (plants, animals, minerals).
- Definition of *priority*—something of leading importance in one's life; what one lives for; the shaping value for one's life.
- The capacity to make decisions and set priorities distinguishes humans from animals, plants, and minerals.
- Discover your priorities—material possessions, money, time?

PREVENIENT GRACE: God loves us and offers a relationship.

- The nature of God is infinitely creative, loving, and good.
- The human situation—created in God's image, fallen from grace through sin, offered salvation in the reconciling work of Jesus Christ.
- God loves us and desires a relationship with us—even more than we desire a relationship with God.
- Definition of *prevenient grace*—God's love pursuing us, awakening and convincing us to come home.
- The loving acts of others communicate God's love to us.
- Personal statement by presenter on how he or she became aware of God's love.

PRIESTHOOD OF ALL BELIEVERS: All believers—laity and clergy alike—are called and given authority to be priests to one another.

- The world does not live in God's grace.

- The answer to the needs of the world is the salvation offered in Jesus Christ.

- Definition of *priesthood of all believers*—A priest acts as God's representative to persons in the world.

- The church consists of people who have experienced God's love and grace and want to share it with others.

- Personal statement by presenter about her or his own experience related to functioning as God's representative to the world.

Permission is granted to duplicate this page.

JUSTIFYING GRACE: The kind of grace at work when we honestly accept the relationship God offers us.

- We all have failed to respond to God's call to place our faith in Jesus Christ alone.
- We are justified when we say yes to the acceptance God offers through Christ: Christ died for us while we were yet sinners.
- The experience of justifying grace is also known as conversion, new birth, being born again, saved from sin, or being born of the Spirit.
- Salvation is both instantaneous and progressive, like two sides of a coin. It involves both justifying grace and sanctifying grace (the topic of the final grace talk).
- Justifying grace enables us to give our hearts to God.
- Personal statement by presenter about his or her own experience of justifying grace.

LIFE OF PIETY: A life lived in relationship with God.

- Prayer is the language we use to communicate with God and to express our relationship with God.
- Scripture provides us with knowledge about the mind, heart, and will of God.
- Characteristics of a life of piety: attention, honesty, authenticity, communication, and resourcefulness.
- Important spiritual practices: prayer, scripture reading, meditation, worship, Communion, and spiritual direction.
- A life of piety has visible qualities that attract others to this kind of life. Such a life is not pious but reflects an awareness of ourselves, others, creation, and God; a desire to fulfill the relationship with God; action (which bears fruit in our decisions and lifestyle); direction (focused on Christ); naturalness (being ourselves); courage; and joy.
- Personal statement by presenter about her or his own experience of living the life of piety.

Permission is granted to duplicate this page.

GROW THROUGH STUDY: Study promotes our movement closer to the realization of Jesus as the model for our lives.

- Definition of *study*—an act or process by which we acquire knowledge of a subject for living. It is not simply an intellectual exercise but a discipline and willingness to inform our desires, emotions, and intuition about the Christian life. The purpose of study is to transform life through the renewal of the mind. (See Romans 12:2.)
- We are either growing or dying. Study helps us continue to grow.
- For a proper perspective, Christians study scripture to know God; we must also study ourselves, others, and the world we live in.
- Both obstacles and aids to study exist.
- The presenter describes his or her own style of study.

MEANS OF GRACE: The sacramental moments in our lives and the ways we corporately celebrate God's grace.

- The sacraments are those acts of worship, instituted by Christ, in which Christ is represented to us in such a way that we experience his presence anew in our lives.
- All Christian traditions recognize baptism and Holy Communion as sacraments.
- Other means of grace include the sacred moments in which Christ is made real for us through symbolic action or ritual at critical points in our lives.
- By grace through faith the Holy Spirit renews our spirits through each and every means of grace.
- Personal statement by presenter about her or his own experience of God's grace through one means of grace.

CHRISTIAN ACTION: Characterizes a Christ-centered life and flows from a relationship with Christ. Christian action bears witness to Christ and carries on his work in all we say and do.

- This process begins when individual lives become Christ-centered.
- We give our hearts to Christ (piety); we give our minds to Christ (study); and we give our hands and feet to Christ (action).
- Christian action is a natural response to God's grace.
- Each person needs a plan of Christian action that starts with friendship.
- Personal statement by presenter about her or his own plan of action.

Permission is granted to duplicate this page.

OBSTACLES TO GRACE: Barriers to a relationship with God; any part of life being presented as the whole.

- Sin is pretending that we are the center of the universe.
- We can overcome sin by practicing the presence of God.
- We put our trust God to overcome obstacles to grace.
- The cross of Christ offers the key to overcoming the obstacles to our relationship with God (vertical) and with our neighbor (horizontal).
- Personal statement by presenter about her or his own experience of overcoming obstacles to grace.

DISCIPLESHIP: Responding fully to the relationship God offers by devoting our life to Christ.

- Serious Christians do not stop short of becoming a disciple.
- Discipleship involves giving our life totally to Christ.
- Disciples seek to glorify God in all they do—with head, heart, and hands.
- A disciple demonstrates these natural qualities: understands priority, has discipline, knows reality, shows empathy, takes initiative, and practices generosity.
- A disciple demonstrates these spiritual qualities: a lively faith, humility, hope, and love.
- Personal statement by presenter about her or his own experience of accountable discipleship.

CHANGING OUR WORLD: Looking at the natural environment and deciding on a plan of action to bring the world to Christ.

- Our first field of ministry is ourselves. Prayer, study, and action change us.
- In the second field of ministry, we bring others to Christ and the church (through prayer, study, and action).
- The third field of ministry is our city, state, and nation (through prayer, study, and action).
- The fourth field of ministry is the other people and nations of the world (through prayer, study, and action).
- Personal statement by presenter of his or her plan of action for each field of ministry.

Permission is granted to duplicate this page.

SANCTIFYING GRACE: The work of the Holy Spirit moves us toward perfection in love and truth.

- Sanctifying grace is the work of the Holy Spirit in rooting out sin—moving us from *imputed* righteousness (what Christ did for us) to *imparted* righteousness (what Christ does in us).
- Definition of sanctifying grace: the process by which the Holy Spirit reveals to us the original righteousness.
- The Holy Spirit indwells and empowers us to love as God loves.
- Sanctifying grace empowers our entire ministry.
- Because God is infinite, our opportunities to grow in grace are also infinite.
- Personal statement by presenter about the work of sanctifying grace in her or his own life.

BODY OF CHRIST: In this talk, pilgrims will come to understand how the church can empower them to be Christ's representatives in the world to the "least of these."

- The primary reason for Emmaus is to strengthen local churches and to develop strong ecumenical leadership to fulfill the Great Commission.
- Definition of *body of Christ*: the entire Christian community in mission to the world.
- The body of Christ must utilize the gifts of all its members to fulfill its mission.
- Characteristics of the body of Christ: alive and life-giving, equipping, intentional in witness, humble in service, confident in Christ's final victory.
- We all need to develop a plan for action that reaches out to "the least of these." (See Matthew 25:45.)
- Personal statement by presenter of how the church has empowered her or him to be Christ's representative in the world.

Permission is granted to duplicate this page.

PERSEVERANCE: This talk explains the need for follow-up and the follow-up system of the Emmaus community (the group reunion and reunion cards).

- Definition of *perseverance*: Continuing to act in the face of difficulty and opposition; to be steadfast in purpose; to press on in the life of grace.
- Pilgrims need to maintain contact with Christ and other Christians.
- The weekly meeting of the group reunion is the premium we pay to persevere in a life of grace.
- Explain group reunions, reunion cards, monthly Gatherings, and Emmaus teams.
- Personal testimony of perseverance by the speaker.

FOURTH DAY: Continues the idea of perseverance in that each succeeding day will be a "fourth day"—every day hereafter for the rest of your life.

- We have experienced God's grace through gifts and sacrifices of the Emmaus Community.
- Our mission now becomes bringing others into a deeper relationship with Christ.
- Pilgrims are sent from the Walk into the world to become a part of the revelation of God's reign. This journey is one of spiritual growth in grace and full participation in God's mission.
- Two dangers: (a) believing you are someone special, and (b) believing you are a nobody.
- We maintain contact with Christ and others, knowing and keeping our priority.
- Personal statement by the speaker of her or his Fourth Day experience.

Permission is granted to duplicate this page.

GENERAL POINTS FOR DISCUSSION AFTER TALKS

PRIORITY

- Humanity's ability to rise above natural impulses and set priorities sets us apart from the rest of creation.

- Our priority determines what life means to us, how we live it, and who we become.

- A true man or woman has an attainable priority toward which to direct his or her life.

- We can discover our real priorities by paying attention to our use of free time, money, and our random thoughts.

PREVENIENT GRACE

- Prevenient grace is God's hidden hand at work from the beginning of our physical life, drawing us to God and to authentic spiritual life.

- We experience prevenient grace through creation, relationships, and Walks; usually we recognize it in retrospect.

- Prevenient grace is the awakening and convincing work of God that brings us to the realization of the difference between formal, external religion and an inward, spiritual relationship with God in Christ.

- God desires a relationship with us even more than we desire a relationship with God.

- God makes us instruments of prevenient grace in other people's lives when we open ourselves to grace.

PRIESTHOOD OF ALL BELIEVERS

- Through our faith and baptism, we all are priests—lay and clergy alike.

- The church is a holy priesthood of people called to act as bridges of grace between God and a world that needs God.

- As priests representing Jesus Christ, we share God's love, grace, and salvation with others.

Permission is granted to duplicate this page.

JUSTIFYING GRACE

- God loves us unconditionally as we are; Christ died for us while we were still sinners.
- While prevenient grace beckons us and convinces us of our need for God, justifying grace moves us to accept the gift of a loving relationship with God as the priority and wellspring for our life.
- Justifying grace enables us to be born again, to be born of the Spirit.
- Acts of agape demonstrate God's love for us through the prayer and sacrifice of others on our behalf.

LIFE OF PIETY

- The life of piety is a life of consciously giving our hearts to God.
- We can nurture our relationship with God through the spiritual discipline of living in God's presence.
- The life of piety is not about being perceived as "holier than thou." Instead, it is about living a devoted, courageous, and joyful Christian life.

GROW THROUGH STUDY

- Through study we give our minds to Christ; regular study helps us live all of life from the mind of Christ.
- If we willingly equip our minds for lesser pursuits, we can equip our minds to fulfill the highest calling.
- A Christian studies the Bible to know how God works in the world; the Christian also studies the world to see how to serve God.

Permission is granted to duplicate this page.

MEANS OF GRACE

- Means of grace are sacred moments and practices in which we come to know, experience, and live in the presence and grace of Christ in the church.

- Means of grace include the sacraments of baptism and Holy Communion, in which Christ makes his saving and sanctifying presence real in our lives.

- God gives us other sacred moments and means of grace to help us live in grace and continue growing as disciples in every phase of our lives.

CHRISTIAN ACTION

- To make Christ real for others, our lives must exemplify an authentic piety.

- Christian action means giving our hands and feet to Christ.

- We can help others know Christ by making friends, being a friend, and sharing with friends our primary relationship—Jesus Christ.

- Each person needs a plan for Christian action.

OBSTACLES TO GRACE

- Despite God's gift of grace and new life in Christ, we can block ourselves from facets of God's grace through many forms of sin.

- Becoming aware of and admitting our obstacles to grace is the first step to overcoming them.

- We overcome all obstacles to our relationship with Christ and with our neighbor through spiritual guidance, daily prayer and repentance, and surrendering anew to God's direction in our lives.

- The cross symbolizes the victory of Jesus Christ over all obstacles to our relationship with God and other people.

Permission is granted to duplicate this page.

DISCIPLESHIP

- Discipleship means fully responding to the call of Christ with heart, head, hands, and feet.
- As disciples, walking with our Lord and growing in his likeness is our highest personal goal.
- Our work is to share Christ and learn to love as Jesus loved.
- Our personal response to Christ's call to discipleship is what these three days are all about.

CHANGING OUR WORLD

- People around us need God's transforming love and vision for life in this world.
- The world is changed whenever we bring Christ's love, truth, justice, and peace to bear in four fields of ministry: (1) ourselves; (2) our family, friends, and church; (3) our city, state, and nation; and (4) other countries and cultures.
- The world is changed whenever we help others realize what it means to be a Christian and to follow Christ.

SANCTIFYING GRACE

- While prevenient grace involves God courting us to bring us to the moment of decision and justifying grace involves God moving us to accept our relationship with God, sanctifying grace involves God's divine energy that enables our growth in relationship with God.
- As we live in obedience to God's call and as we practice the means of grace, the Holy Spirit empowers us to love as Jesus loved and to mature in the likeness of Christ.
- We do not preoccupy ourselves with growth in goodness but focus upon our call to humble service to Christ in the world.

Permission is granted to duplicate this page.

BODY OF CHRIST

- The body of Christ is the community of disciples who offer their lives to continue Christ's ministry in the world.

- God has given gifts to every member of the body of Christ; we need to call forth and exercise these gifts.

- We work together to build up the church, to form living Christian communities, and to show forth Christ's life of love in definitive ways so that the world may believe.

- The true measure of the effectiveness of the body of Christ is how it cares for "the least of these." (See Matthew 25:45.)

PERSEVERANCE

- As disciples, we are called to persevere in grace for the rest of our lives.

- The struggle to bring God's justice and peace to "the least of these" and to the systems in which they live requires perseverance.

- Emmaus group reunions offer an effective way to persevere and grow in grace.

- The key to perseverance is regular weekly attendance of worship and group reunions, commitment to supporting one another, hold one another accountable, and offer guidance.

FOURTH DAY

- We are sent out to be Christ's apostles in today's world.

- We will encounter obstacles, but we can overcome them through contact with Christ and other Christians.

- Emmaus community Gatherings, group reunions, other Emmaus involvement, and the local church provide the necessary support.

- We have shared three wonderful days in grace. Now we are sent to live the rest of our lives as a Fourth Day, as a continuing Walk to Emmaus with Christ.

Permission is granted to duplicate this page.

PREPARING TABLE LEADERS AND ASSISTANT TABLE LEADERS

The Table Leader holds the most influential job in the conference room. A Table Leader can make all the difference in a person's experience of the event, for better or for worse. So Table Leaders deserve sufficient orientation and training for their role.

A previous section in this manual included information about the roles of the Table Leader and Assistant Table Leader. Here are more helpful resources:

- Talk preview discussions in small groups during team meetings can provide the opportunity for team members to practice guiding a small-group discussion.

- A well-planned team discussion on the role of the Table Leader and on keys to effective table leadership can elicit a wealth of insight from team members on helpful table leadership.

- A Table Leader and Assistant Table Leader training workshop that includes presentation, discussion, and role play during a team meeting can be a valuable tool. Teams for a pair of Walks come together for one hour (assuming the teams meet simultaneously).

- The *Walk to Emmaus Team Manual* devotes a chapter to table leadership. Every Table Leader and Assistant Table Leader will study and discuss this chapter during team training.

- Duplicate and distribute copies of "The Importance of the Table Leader" (from the "Team Meeting Forms and Handouts" section) to remind Table Leaders of their responsibilities and the necessary leadership style.

PREPARING MUSIC DIRECTORS

Music Directors can prepare themselves and the team by leading singing during team meetings and teaching the team important songs. Worship times during team meetings offer opportunities to try out potential music for the Walk. A brief discussion on team members' experiences of good music leadership can encourage and strengthen the Music Directors. In addition, every Music Director will have in hand the Checklist for Music Directors (see the "Music Directors" section in this manual) and be prepared to share the traditions behind "De Colores" and the singing of grace before and after meals. The Lay and Spiritual Directors meet with the Music Directors to make sure they share common expectations for their roles during the three days and to plan times for music on the Walk.

TEAM MEETING SCHEDULES

Before the first team meeting, the Board of Directors conducts an orientation that covers team responsibilities, support committee responsibilities, an overview of Emmaus, and the plan for team formation. After the final team meeting, a potluck fellowship with spouses may be held. This meeting could include a commissioning service, Communion, and last-minute reminders.

Team formation schedules include enough time to preview all the talks and build the team—a total of twenty-three to twenty-six meeting hours. The hours of team meeting derives from the various functions team members are to accomplish. It takes approximately one hour to preview one of the regular talks. Previewing the MEANS OF GRACE talk will require two hours. These previews generate sixteen hours of team meetings. The opening worship and floating accountability group time will take approximately thirty minutes for each meeting. Team training conducted at each session accounts for approximately three hours. Community building and team building will generate another three hours of time distributed over the meetings. Each Community works out a schedule that best suits its situation to meet the goals of team formation, whether it uses one of the recommended schedules below or some combination of them.

Option 1: Eight to ten weekly meetings. This schedule employs weekly meetings of approximately three hours each. This plan especially suits Communities in which team members live, work, or attend school close enough to one another to make weekly evening meetings possible. An extended number of meetings gives the team time to grow together gradually. This schedule also gives the event team leaders plenty of time to notice and respond to needs among the team members.

Option 2: This schedule consists of four all-day meetings of about six hours each. This schedule especially suits Communities in which team members must drive long distances to meetings, which makes successive weekly and evening meetings difficult. This schedule requires four talk previews for each meeting (one meeting will have three talk previews. Seasoned team members can preview their talks at the first meeting to serve as a model for new team members. Other than requiring the preview of more talks at each meeting, the elements of each session follow the description above.

Option 3: This schedule consists of two meetings each starting on Friday evening and ending on Saturday evening (meeting hours would be roughly 7–10 p.m. on Friday, and 9 a.m.–5 p.m. on Saturday). Each meeting may require that some team members spend the night. The team members living close enough to go home Friday night could graciously host those who cannot return home overnight. This schedule again provides all the elements of the team meetings. To make better use of the available time, make meal arrangements in advance.

SECTION 13— TEAM MEETING FORMS AND HANDOUTS

TEAM WORKSHEET FOR _____ WALK TO EMMAUS # _____

This sample worksheet is based on thirty-six pilgrims with six tables (six pilgrims per table) plus one Table Leader and one Assistant Table Leader. The Conference Room Team consists of twenty-four persons.

Leaders' Table	
Lay Director	_____
Asst. Lay Director	_____
Asst. Lay Director	_____
Asst. Lay Director	_____
Spiritual Director	_____
Asst. Spiritual Director	_____
Asst. Spiritual Director	_____
Asst. Spiritual Director	_____
Asst. Spiritual Director	_____
Music Director	_____
Asst. Music Director	_____
Board Representative	_____

Permission is granted to duplicate this page.

Table Leaders

Table	Table Leader	Assistant Table Leader
_____	_____	_____
_____	_____	_____
_____	_____	_____
_____	_____	_____
_____	_____	_____
_____	_____	_____

Emmaus Talks

PRIORITY (ALD)	_____
PREVENIENT GRACE (ASD)	_____
PRIESTHOOD OF ALL BELIEVERS (TL/ATL)	_____
JUSTIFYING GRACE (ASD)	_____
LIFE OF PIETY (TL/ATL)	_____
MEANS OF GRACE (SD)	_____
CHRISTIAN ACTION (TL/ATL)	_____
Obstacles to Grace (ASD)	_____
DISCIPLESHIP (TL/ATL)	_____
CHANGING OUR WORLD (TL/ATL)	_____
SANCTIFYING GRACE (ASD)	_____
BODY OF CHRIST (TL/ATL)	_____
PERSEVERANCE (LD)	_____
Fourth Day (ALD)	_____

Key to Abbreviations

ALD = Assistant Lay Director
ASD = Assistant Spiritual Director
TL = Table Leader
ATL = Assistant Table Leader
SD = Spiritual Director
LD = Lay Director

Permission is granted to duplicate this page.

THE IMPORTANCE OF THE TABLE LEADER

Why am I here, Lord?

- I'm here to praise God and to do God's holy work here on earth.

- I'm here to imitate Jesus Christ and to be a window through which the love and grace of Christ can be seen by the pilgrims at this Walk to Emmaus.

- I'm here to pray and make sacrifices for the entire team and pilgrims.

- I'm here to help establish a Christian community by bringing Jesus Christ to this team and pilgrims by accepting the gift of the Holy Spirit.

- I'm here to know the intent of the talks and to help each speaker accomplish the aim of his or her talk by guiding and directing discussion at the table.

- I'm here to display Christian discipleship—to demonstrate love and show my concern for others and accept other persons as individuals.

- I'm here to demonstrate leadership not domination. I do not seek glory for myself but act from loving concern. I'm here as a guide not a counselor. I'm here to listen and to ensure that every person at the table has opportunity to speak.

- I'm here so that when these three days are over, the pilgrims will be able to say of the team members, "I came looking for Christ and found Christ at my table."

- I'm here to ask humbly that God's will, not my will, be done.

- Christ, I'm here to submit my heart and soul to you so your love will grow in me and in each person at my table.

- In all situations I shall ask, "What would Jesus do?"

Permission is granted to duplicate this page.

SCHEDULE OF TALKS FOR TEAM MEETINGS

Day One

Theme: God freely offers grace to all, and those who respond live a life of love.

Date and time to preview talk	Title of talk	Person giving talk
_____	PRIORITY	_____
_____	PREVENIENT GRACE	_____
_____	PRIESTHOOD OF ALL BELIEVERS	_____
_____	JUSTIFYING GRACE	_____
_____	LIFE OF PIETY	_____

Day Two

Theme: Christ is the message God sent to the world. We are invited to accept a relationship with God through Jesus Christ.

Date and time to preview talk	Title of talk	Person giving talk
_____	GROW THROUGH STUDY	_____
_____	MEANS OF GRACE	_____
_____	CHRISTIAN ACTION	_____
_____	OBSTACLES TO GRACE	_____
_____	DISCIPLESHIP	_____

Permission is granted to duplicate this page.

Day Three

Theme: "Go therefore and make disciples of all nations" (Matt. 28:19).

Date and time to preview talk	Title of talk	Person giving talk
_____	CHANGING OUR WORLD	_____
_____	SANCTIFYING GRACE	_____
_____	BODY OF CHRIST	_____
_____	Perseverance	_____
_____	FOURTH DAY	_____

Permission is granted to duplicate this page.

TEAM MEETING PRAYER PARTNER SHEET

Team Member	Team Member

Permission is granted to duplicate this page.

TEAM MEETING SUPPLY LIST

_____   Bell(s)

_____   Name tags (for team members who do not have one)

_____   Pencils/pens

_____   Team roster

_____   Copy of the manual checkout sheet (if applicable)

_____   Copy of team attendance sheet

_____   Roster of participants

_____   Copies of *The Walk to Emmaus Team Manual* (one per team member)

_____   Paper for taking notes

_____   Songbooks (check with Music Directors)

_____   Communion elements (check with Spiritual Director)

_____   Lectern (if the facility does not have one)

_____   Bible, cross to set on table, candle and matches (if allowed), cross for speaker to hold

_____   Microphone/sound system (if needed)

_____   Ice chest, coffee pot, etc.

Permission is granted to duplicate this page.

WALK TO EMMAUS TEAM MANUAL CHECKOUT SHEET

Walk # _____

Name	Manual #	Date Out	Initials	Date In	Initials
1.					
2.					
3.					
4.					
5.					
6.					
7.					
8.					
9.					
10.					
11.					
12.					
13.					
14.					
15.					
16.					
17.					
18.					
19.					
20.					
21.					
22.					
23.					
24.					
25.					
26.					

Permission is granted to duplicate this page.

WALK TO EMMAUS TEAM CANON

It's Not about Me!

- I am a member of an Emmaus team; therefore, I am only one part of a complete being.

- I am an imperfect earthen vessel, and I am blessed to be here in a servant's role.

- I will serve in humility and gratitude for the opportunity to be here and will remember that the Holy Spirit calls for my love, patience, kindness, gentleness, and self-control in all things.

- I will pray for submission to the Holy Spirit and for strength and commitment to be God's person rather than my own person during this time.

- I will remember that I am here only as an instrument through which God can work to renew the church.

- I am here only by God's grace and only so that the Holy Spirit might work through me.

- I will lift up other team members and pilgrims in prayer and ask our Lord to strengthen them and open their eyes so that we all might recognize Jesus Christ in the breaking of the bread.

- I will not overstate or overemphasize my role by any word or deed.

- I will not glorify myself; I will not glorify any other team member nor allow another to glorify me.

- I will remember that the pilgrims are the main reason for my presence and my prayers.

- I will remember at all times that I am no more important than any other person with whom I am sharing this experience.

- In all things, I will accept and obey the authority and discipline under which I serve.

- I have no authority or responsibility except to obey God and to respond to the ministry of the Holy Spirit.

- Whatever passions and excitement seize me, I will express them through joyful praise to God, my Lord Jesus Christ, and the Holy Spirit.

- I will give God all the glory for whatever happens during this time together.

- I will raise my voice only to praise God and will bow my head in reverence and submission to God.

- I am only a servant, but God can use me more powerfully in this role than in any other role I might choose.

- I am a member of an Emmaus team; in all things, I pray that Christ will be lifted up.

Permission is granted to duplicate this page.

WALK TO EMMAUS TEAM ATTENDANCE SHEET

Walk #_____

Team Members / Dates								

Permission is granted to duplicate this page.

EXPLANATIONS FOR THE TEAM BEFORE THE WALK TO EMMAUS

1. Explain the Send-Off procedures (making announcements, calling out individual names, and noting whether applause is encouraged). The Lay Director calls out individual names, mixing the names of Conference Room Team members and pilgrims. As each person hears his or her name called, the person repeats his or her name and joins the Lay Director at the designated lineup place.

2. Explain the procedure by which table assignments are made on Friday morning, how Table Leaders and Assistant Table Leaders are introduced, and how rotation works at the tables before each talk.

    *   The Table Leader sits at the table with his or her back to the speaker. The Assistant Table Leader sits directly across from the Table Leader. These two persons do not rotate seats. All other members rotate seats before each talk.

    *   Introduce Table Leaders and Assistant Table Leaders as the tables are assigned. Explain that the Assistant Table Leader will serve as the secretary for the first talk; that responsibility will rotate among all table members.

    *   When team members call out their names and table name during these three days, they refer to their table assignment for this particular Walk.

3. Explain how Assistant Lay Directors will notify each speaker to dress and proceed to the chapel, introduce each talk, set up the speaker's visual aids, and lead each speaker into the conference room.

4. Remind everyone that the Assistant Lay Directors are responsible for keeping up with medicines and/or the times for persons to take medications, since pilgrims are asked to remove their watches.

5. After most talks, the speakers close with the words *De Colores*. The speakers then return to the Prayer chapel for prayer.

6. An Assistant Lay Director then announces to the group, "Please bow for a moment of silent meditation."

7. Tell about the distribution of general agape, beginning with the agape explanation during the JUSTIFYING GRACE talk. All pilgrims receive equal amounts of agape: one piece of a kind per person in the dining hall and on beds. No agape or gifts are distributed to particular persons from sponsors, spouses, parents, or friends. These items are held for pilgrims as they return home.

8. The reunion card will be introduced at the end of the SANCTIFYING GRACE talk. The Lay Director explains the practice of the reunion card during the PERSEVERANCE talk. Tables will actually use the reunion card in small groups in the discussion time following the PERSEVERANCE talk. Table Leaders and Assistant Table Leaders model the sharing through the use of the card.

9. Team members wear Emmaus crosses beginning with the Commissioning on Sunday afternoon and also may wear them during their talk.

10. Walk through team members' participation at Closing.

    *   The whole team will be introduced by the role in which they served during the three days (such as Table Leaders, Assistant Table Leaders, etc.).

    *   Remind them that two team members will share their answers to the two closing questions with the group: "What has this weekend meant to me?" and "What do I intend to do about it?"

    *   Remind everyone that the invitation to share at Closing is addressed only to the pilgrims.

11. Hand out table assignments to Table Leaders/Assistant Table Leaders so they can pray for their table members before the Walk begins

Prayer to the Holy Spirit

Come, Holy Spirit, fill the hearts of your faithful and kindle in us the fire of your love. Send forth your Spirit, and we shall be created.

And you shall renew the face of the earth.

O God, who by the light of the Holy Spirit did instruct the hearts of the faithful, grant that by the same Holy Spirit we may be truly wise and ever enjoy your consolations.

Through Christ our Lord. Amen.

Introduction for Each Talk

With a clean sheet of paper, high idealism, the spirit of cooperation and charity, and pen in hand, prepare for the next talk, which will be given by a clergyperson/layperson.

Permission is granted to duplicate this page.

TABLE ROSTER

1. Table of	2. Table of	3. Table of
TL:	TL:	TL:
ATL:	ATL:	ATL:

4. Table of	5. Table of	6. Table of
TL:	TL:	TL:
ATL:	ATL:	ATL:

Permission is granted to duplicate this page.

THEMES ACROSS THE DAYS

The first talk of each day focuses on the decisions we need to make.

PRIORITY	What will I do with my life?
GROWTH THROUGH STUDY	On what or whom will I base my life?
CHANGING OUR WORLD	What difference do I want to make in this world?

The second talk focuses on the theme of that day.

PREVENIENT GRACE	God's grace envelops us.
MEANS OF GRACE	Ways I receive and live in grace.
SANCTIFYING GRACE	Ways I can grow toward holiness and embody grace.

The third talk focuses on the ways Christians serve.

PRIESTHOOD OF ALL BELIEVERS	Sharing grace with others.
CHRISTIAN ACTION	Sharing Christ with others.
BODY OF CHRIST	Sharing with all members of the Christian community in the ministry and mission of Christ.

The fourth talk focuses on individual responses to the themes.

JUSTIFYING GRACE	How do you respond to God's grace? (I accept.)
OBSTACLES OF GRACE	How do you respond to impediments to a life of grace? (Sometimes I stand, sometimes I fall; always I take up the cross.)
PERSEVERANCE	What will you do to continue living in grace? (Participate regularly in group reunions, Gatherings, the local church, and global missions.)

The fifth talk focuses on our lifestyle.

PIETY	Living a life of devotion to God.
DISCIPLESHIP	Committing to being Christ in the church and world.
FOURTH DAY	Persevering in grace.

Permission is granted to duplicate this page.

THREE-DAY OVERVIEW

Day 1	Day 2	Day 3
God Proclamation/Call Divine Invitation	*The Lord Jesus Christ* Conversion Our Response	*The Holy Spirit* Consecration Christian Life in Mission
Morning Meditation **THE LOVING FATHER** **(Prodigal Son)** God loves us unconditionally and longs for our return.	**Morning Meditation** **FOUR RESPONSES TO CHRIST** In view of these, how will we respond to Christ?	**Morning Meditation** **HUMANNESS OF JESUS** God uses our humanness to touch this world with grace.
PRIORITY Human beings are shaped by a unique capacity to make decisions about their priorities. What is your priority?	**GROW THROUGH GRACE** New life in Christ involves growing through study of scripture, tradition, and our world (giving our mind to God).	**CHANGING OUR WORLD** Disciples will transform their environments by being a Christian presence in the four fields of ministry.
PREVENIENT GRACE God's love searches us out, seeks to redeem humanity, and wants to give us a life in grace.	**MEANS OF GRACE** This new life in Christ is made real by means of sacraments and other sacred moments in which we celebrate Christ's overcoming death in our lives.	**SANCTIFYING GRACE** Disciples continue to grow in the grace of Christ through obedience to the Holy Spirit in the disciplines of prayer and service.
PRIESTHOOD OF ALL BELIEVERS God's love is shared by Christians called to be the church—to be priests to one another, a channel of grace between God and people.	**CHRISTIAN ACTION** This new life is expressed by sharing Christ as a friend with friends—giving hands and feet to God, both in the church and in the world.	**BODY OF CHRIST** Disciples are called together to be the body of Christ, joining their gifts for ministry and mission to "the least of these."

Permission is granted to duplicate this page.

Day 1	Day 2	Day 3
JUSTIFYING GRACE By God's grace, we are accepted and set right with God in Jesus Christ. New life in Christ comes when we say yes to God's offer of grace.	**OBSTACLES OF GRACE** This new life is not free from obstacles of sin, but grace and discipline enable us to overcome obstacles and grow through them.	**PERSEVERANCE** Disciples of Jesus cannot make it alone but can persevere with strength from the Spirit through mutual support in accountability groups.
LIFE OF PIETY This new life is rooted in a living relationship with God, sustained by grace through spiritual disciplines—giving our heart to God.	**DISCIPLESHIP** This new life is discipleship, life lived in grace, following in Jesus' footsteps, growing in his likeness—giving heart, head, and hands to God.	**FOURTH DAY** The three days are over, but Day Four begins. This is Emmaus's purpose: a lifetime of discipleship, bringing new life to our churches and conveying grace where we live.
Day 1 Focus God graciously offer s us a relationship and a new life centered in Jesus Christ.	**Day 2 Focus** Christ models our response to that gracious offer and our living in grace as disciples through practicing the means of grace.	**Day 3 Focus** The Holy Spirit has a strategy for bringing new life and transformation to our world through us and our ongoing participation in that mission as the church.

Permission is granted to duplicate this page.

CPSIA information can be obtained
at www.ICGtesting.com
Printed in the USA
LVHW052027200219
608259LV00004B/5